George H. Thurston

Thurston's Route Book from Philadelphia to Chicago

Via Pennsylvania Central Railroad and Pittsburgh, Fort Wayne & Chicago

Railway

George H. Thurston

Thurston's Route Book from Philadelphia to Chicago
Via Pennsylvania Central Railroad and Pittsburgh, Fort Wayne & Chicago Railway

ISBN/EAN: 9783337146429

Printed in Europe, USA, Canada, Australia, Japan

Cover: Foto ©Lupo / pixelio.de

More available books at **www.hansebooks.com**

GENERAL TIME SCHEDULE,

From New York, Philadelphia and Baltimore.

GOING WEST.				GOING EAST.		

VIA ALLENTOWN. / VIA ALLENTOWN.

MAIL.	EXPRESS.	EXPRESS.			EXPRESS.	EXPRESS.	MAIL.
12 00 M.	7 00 P. M.	6 00 A. M.	Le	New York..........	Arr. 10 30 P. M.	9 35 A. M.	5 50 P. M.
8 20 P. M.	2 00 A. M.	1 15 P. M.	"	Harrisburg	" 12 45 P. M.	1 45 "	5 40 A. M.
	7 15 "	7 15 "	"	Altoona.............	" 7 40 A. M.	8 40 P. M.	1 10 "
	12 00 M.	12 30 A. M.	Arr.	Pittsburgh	Le. 3 00 A. M.	4 00 "	8 45 P. M.

VIA PHILADELPHIA. / VIA PHILADELPHIA.

					EXPRESS.	EXPRESS.	EXPRESS.
	6 00 P. M.	7 00 A. M.	Le.	New York..........	Arr. 9 30 P. M.	12 00 M.	2 30 P. M.
7 30 A. M.	10 30 "	11 30 "	"	Philadelphia.......	" 5 20 "	6 30 A. M.	10 15 A. M
1 15 P. M.	3 00 A. M	3 50 P. M.	"	Harrisburg	" 12 45 "	1 45 "	5 40 "
7 15 "	8 00 "	8 35 "	"	Altoona......·.....	" 7 40 A. M.	8 40 P. M	1 10 "
12 30 A. M.	12 30 P. M.	1 00 A. M.	Arr.	Pittsburgh	Le. 3 00 "	4 00 "	8 45 P. M

VIA BALTIMORE. / VIA BALTIMORE.

	6 30 P. M.	6 30 A. M.	Le.	Washington City,	Arr. 9 35 P. M.	9 50 A. M.	5 25 P. M.
2 55 P. M.	9 15 "	9 15 "	"	Baltimore...........	" 5 35 "	6 15 "	11 30 A. M.
7 30 "	2 00 A. M.	1 15 P. M.	"	Harrisburg	" 12 45 "	1 45 "	5 40 "
	7 15 "	7 15 "	"	Altoona.............	" 7 40 A. M.	8 40 P. M.	1 10 "
	12 00 M.	12 30 A. M.	Arr.	Pittsburgh	Le. 3 00 "	4 00 "	8 45 P. M.

TO CHICAGO. / FROM CHICAGO.

7 00 A. M.	12 40 P. M.	1 00 A. M.	Le.	Pittsburgh	Arr. 2 25 A. M.	3 05 P. M.	7 50 P. M.
11 20 "	4 10 "	4 10 "	"	Alliance............	" 11 10 P. M.	11 20 A. M.	4 30 "
6 00 P. M	8 15 "	8 00 "	Arr.	Crestline............	" 6 50 "	6 45 "	1 12 "
12 00 M.	2 10 A. M.	2 10 P. M.	"	Fort Wayne.......	Le. 1 15 "	1 20 "	
9 10 P. M.	7 40 "	7 15 "	"	Chicago.............	" 7 20 A. M.	7 15 P. M.	
		9 15 P. M	10 05 A. M.	"	St. Louis, via Chi.		

TO CINCINNATI AND ST. LOUIS. / FROM ST. LOUIS AND CINCINNATI.

	8 40 P. M.	8 30 A. M.	Le.	Crestline......	Arr. 6 35 P. M.	6 35 A. M.	1 05 P. M.
	11 15 "	10 45 "	Arr	Columbus	Le. 3 45 "	4 00 "	11 10 A. M.
	5 55 A. M.	3 50 P. M.	"	Cincinnati	" 10 15 P. M.	10 15 P. M.	7 00 "
	12 30 P. M.	12 15 A. M.	"	Louisville...........	" 10 00 P. M.	2 45 "	
	10 40 "	10 00 "	"	St. Louis............	" 4 45 "	7 00 A. M.	

TO INDIANAPOLIS AND ST. LOUIS. / FROM ST. LOUIS AND INDIANAPOLIS.

	8 45 P. M.	8 30 A. M.	Le	Crestline............	Arr.	6 30 A. M.	1 00 P. M.
	6 00 A. M	6 00 P. M.	Arr	Indianapolis.......	Le.	8 15 P. M.	5 00 A. M.
	12 30 P. M.	12 15 A. M.	"	Louisville	"	2 45 "	10 00 P. M.
	7 00 "	8 15 "	"	St. Louis......... ...	"	6 30 A. M.	4 55 "

ROUTE BOOK.

The Pennsylvania Rail Road

AND THE

Pittsburgh, Ft. Wayne & Chicogo Railway,

FORM THE SHORTEST ROUTE

From NEW YORK (via either Philadelphia or the Allentown Route) PHILA-
DELPHIA or BALTIMORE, to CHICAGO, ST. LOUIS, CAIRO,
and all the cities and towns of the West and North-West.

There being but ONE CHANGE OF CARS between New York and Chicago
(via Allentown and Pittsburgh), but two changes via Philadelphia, but one
change between Philadelphia and Chicago, and two changes from Baltimore,
with Woodruff's celebrated sleeping cars on all night trains, the passenger
will find the *shortest line* combined with the *greatest comfort* by taking this
route.

THE

GREAT MIDDLE ROUTE

From New York to the West,

Known as the ALLENTOWN ROUTE, is the SHORTEST, in both distance and
time, from New York to Cincinnati, St. Louis or Chicago, being 60 miles
shorter and the time TWO HOURS quicker than by any of the northern routes.

Passengers by this route leave New York at the foot of Courtlandt street
by the ferry to Jersey City. The route runs via Newark and Elizabeth, and
the Central Railway of New Jersey, to Easton, at the junction of the Lehigh
with the Delaware River. Thence over the Lehigh Valley R. R., following
the banks of the Lehigh River, to Allentown, and over the East Penn'a R. R.
to Reading, and from that point over the Lebanon Valley branch of the Philadelphia & Reading R. R. to Harrisburgh, where it connects with the Great
Pennsylvania Rail Road to Pittsburgh.

The scenery of this route is not excelled on the continent. From the beautifully cultivated fields and gentle slopes of New Jersey and the Lebanon Valley, to the wild and scenic grandeur of the Juniata and Alleghenies, the
transition is so gradual, and yet so swift, as to compress into a seventeen
hours' ride, a variety of beauties of nature, formerly attainable only by a tour
of weeks or months.

To business men, its advantages are greatest; allowing them to transact
a full day's business in New York, they can leave there in the 7 00 P. M.
train, take a sleeping car, and after a refreshing sleep and good breakfast at
Altoona, arrive in Pittsburgh at noon, without having changed cars. The
train to Chicago, leaving in just one hour, allows ample time for dinner, and
again a ride of 468 miles, without any change of cars, brings them to that
commercial metropolis of the West.

(3)

To ladies, traveling alone, the route offers peculiar facilities from the very few changes of cars; to all, it is the *shortest*, QUICKEST, BEST, and we express unqualifiedly the opinion, that every one who once travels it, will never go by any other, unless called by his engagements to stop at a point on some other route.

The *Camden & Amboy and New York R. R. Route*, via Philadelphia, is the next in time and distance, from New York to the West.

There are two distinct roads from N. Y. to Phila. The *New Jersey R. R.* leaving at the foot of Courtlandt St., on ferry to Jersey City, and thence via Newark, New Brunswick and Trenton, to Kenningston District, Phila. The *Camden & Amboy* leaving at foot of Barclay St., by boat to Amboy, and thence via Bordentown and Camden to Walnut St. wharf, Phila. Some trains run by New Jersey R. R. as above to Trenton, thence by branch R. R. to Bordentown and into Phila. via Camden.

THE GREAT CENTRAL ROUTE
From Philadelphia,

which this publication verbally illustrates, is of great attraction to the tourist, and of equally great importance to the business man. Passing through the heart of the great commonwealth of Pennsylvania, from its eastern borders to its western, it carries the traveler over and by some of the most famous scenes of our colonial and revolutionary history, and by points celebrated in the traditions of the red man. Traversing some of the finest agricultural counties in the Keystone State, the route penetrates the heart of the coal and iron producing region, and conveys the traveler through the grandest and most picturesque of mountain scenery.

Leaving the Keystone State, the route runs through the famous wheat district of Ohio, and traverses the most noted agricultural section of the Buckeye State, passing many spots renowned in the history of the early settlement of the great North-Western Territory, and the Indian wars of that period.

After traversing the entire breadth of the State of Ohio, it enters the State of Indiana, across the northern portion, passing in its course the sites of famous Indian villages, border battles, and frontier forts, affording fine views of the scenery of the Hoosier State, with its flourishing villages and extensive farms. From Indiana the route passes into the State of Illinois, giving views of its broad prairies, and occasionally of the blue waters of Lake Michigan, until the traveler is safely landed in the renowned city of Chicago.

By this route (which is shorter by 60 miles than any other between New York and Chicago or St. Louis,) the traveler is conveyed 898 miles, with but one change of cars, over and through the territory of five states. Traversing in those states 42 Counties, containing manufacturing, agricultural and mining populations; running through three of the chief cities of the Union, each famous for the specialities of its business; affording views of many of the chief inland towns of the five states, it thus presents to the eye of the traveler a greater variety of scenery, population, and business, than is passed in any other route.

TIME TABLE PENNSYLVANIA CENTRAL RAILROAD.

Trains going West leave Stations as follows:

	Balti. Exp. A. M.	Phila. Exp. P. M.	Fast Line. A. M.	Mail. A. M.		Balt. Exp. A. M.	Phila. Exp. A. M.	Fast Line. P. M.	Mail. P. M.
PHILAD'A....		10 30	11 30	7 30	Cove	2 23	3 23	4 13	1-43
W. Philad'a...		10 45	11 40	7 40	Duncannon....	2 32	3 32	4 22	1 53
City Avenue..		10 56	11 50	7 55	Aqueduct Sid.	2 38	3 38	4 28	2 02
White Hall....		11 07	12 00	8 10	Baily's	2 48	3 47	4 37	2 14
			P. M.		Newport........	3 00	4 00	4 49	2 27
Morgans Cor'r		11 15	12 07	8 19	Millerstown ...	3 10	4 09	4 58	2 42
Eagle............		11 21	12 1	8 28	Thompsont'n..	3 20	4 18	5 07	2 55
Paoli............		11 30	12	0	Tuscarora......	3 30	4 27	5 16	3 08
Westchest'r In		11 34	12	45	Perrysville.....	3 38	4 34	5 22	3 16
Steamboat.....		11 42	12 33	8 56	Mifflin	3 45	4 40	5 28	3 23
Oakland		11 49	12 40	9 06	"Narrows,"....	3 57	4 51	5 39	3 38
Downingtown		11 59	1 05	9 18	Lewistown.....	4 11	5 05	5 51	3 51
		A. M.			End D'ble T'k	4 14	5 07	5 53	3 54
Gallagherville		12 02	1 08	9 22	Anderson's S..	4 27	5 20	6 05	4 09
Coatesville		12 14	1 20	9 35	M'Veytown....	4 37	5 29	6 14	4 21
Chandler's		12 21	1 27	9 41	Manayunk Sid.	4 46	5 38	6 23	4 32
Parkesburg ...		12 25	1 30	9 48	N. Hamilton...	4 57	5 48	6 33	4 46
Penningtonv'e		12 31	1 36	9 57	Mount Union..	5 05	5 56	6 39	4 54
Christiana......		12 34	1 39	10 02	Mill Creek......	5 20	6 09	6 52	5 09
Gap.............		12 40	1 44	10 09	Huntingdon ...	5 33	6 22	7 05	5 23
Kinzer's........		12 46	1 50	10 17	Petersburg....	5 47	6 36	7 18	5 39
Leaman Place		12 55	1 58	10 27	Barree	5 54	6 43	7 25	5 48
Gordonville ...		12 58	2 01	10 30	Spruce Creek.	6 00	6 49	7 30	5 54
Bird-in-Hand.		1 05	2 08	10 38	Birmingham...	6 13	7 02	7 43	6 10
Lancaster......		1 21	2 23	10 55	Tyrone	6 21	7 10	7 50	6 19
Dillerville......		1 25	2 26	10 58	Tipton	6 31	7 19	7 58	6 30
Landisville		1 38	2 40		Fostoria	6 35	7 23	8 02	6 35
Mount Joy.....		1 48	2 49		Bell's Mills.....	6 39	7 27	8 05	6 40
Kuhnz's Sid'g		1 55	2 56		Altoona.........	7 15	8 00	8 35	7 15
Elizabethtown		2 03	3 05		Kittanning Pt.	7 30	8 13	8 45	7 30
Conewago Sid.		2 12	3 12		East End Tun'l	7 45	8 28	9 00	7 45
				P. M.	Gallitzin........	7 50	8 33	9 05	7 50
Branch Inter'n		2 23	3 22	12 17	Cresson.........	7 58	8 40	9 11	7 58
Middletown ...		2 25	3 25	12 20	Lillys............	8 05	8 47	9 17	8 05
Highspire......		2 32	3 32	12 30	Portage.........	8 14	8 56	9 26	8 16
Harrisburg....	2 00	3 00	3 50	1 15	Wilmore........	8 21	9 03	9 32	8 25
Rockv'e Sw'ch	2 10	3 10	4 00	1 27	Summerhill ...	8 27	9 08	9 37	8 31
Sid W. of b'ge	2 15	3 15	4 05	1 32	S. Fork.........	8 32	9 12	9 41	8 36
N. C. Crossing	2 18	3 18	4 08	1 36					

[CONTINUED ON PAGE 4.]

TIME TABLE PENNSYLVANIA CENTRAL RAILROAD.

Trains going East leave Stations as follows:

LEAVES	Express P. M.	Fast P. M.	Mail A. M.		Express P. M.	Fast A. M.	Mail A. M.
PITTSBURG .	4 00	8 45	3 00	Altoona.........	8 40	1 15	8 00
Outer Station.	4 10	8 55	3 10	Bells' Mills....	9 14	1 30	8 14
East Liberty...	4 17	9 02	3 17	Fostoria........	9 18	1 15	8 18
Wilkinsburg...	4 22	9 06	3 22	Tipton	9 23	1 34	8 23
Brinton's.......	4 32	9 15	3 32	Tyrone..........	9 33	1 42	8 33
Turtle Creek..	4 35	9 17	3 85	........am...	9 41	1 49	8 41
Walls..........	4 38	9 20	3 38	........reek.	9 54	2 02	8 54
Stewart's	4 43	9 25	3 43	....	9 59	2 07	8 59
Irwin's..........	4 53	9 35	3 53	Petersburg.....	10 06	2 13	9 06
Manor	4 57	9 39	3 57	Huntingdon ...	10 21	2 27	9 21
Penn Station..	5 00	9 42	4 00	Mill Creek......	10 31	2 38	9 31
Radebaugh's...	5 08	9 49	4 08	Mount Union.	10 45	2 50	9 45
Greensburg....	5.14	9 54	4 14	N. Hamilton...	10 52	2 56	9 52
George's........	5 21	10 01	4 21	Manayunk Sid.	11 04	3 06	10 04
Beatty's.........	5 30	10 10	4 30	M'Veytown....	11 13	3 15	10 13
Latrobe.........	5 37	10 15	4 37	Anderson's S..	11 22	3 24	10 22
Derry............	5 47	10 25	4 47	End Double T.	11 37	3 36	10 37
Hillside.........	5 55	10 32	4 55	Lewistown.....	11 40	3 39	10 40
Blairsville Br..	6 03	10 40	5 02	"Narrows,"....	11 51	3 49	10 50
Bolivar	6 13	10 49	5 12		A. M.		
Lockport.......	6 16	10 52	5 15	Mifflin..........	12 05	4 01	11 05
New Florence.	6 25	11 00	5 24	Perrysville.....	12 11	4 06	11 10
Nineveh	6 33	11 08	5 33	Tuscarora......	12 18	4 13	11 18
Slackwater S..	6 41	11 16	5 41	Thompsont'n..	12 28	4 22	11 28
Cambria Sid'g	6 50	11 25	5 50	Millerstown....	12 38	4 31	11 38
Johnstown.....	6 55	11 30	5 55	Newport........	12 49	4 43	11 49
Conemaugh ...	7 00	11 35	6 00	Baily's	12 58	4 52	11 58
Cross'g Swit'h	7 02	11 37	6 02				P. M.
Mineral Point.	7 11	11 46	6 11	Aqueduct Sid.	1 08	5 02	12 08
S. Fork.........	7 17	11 51	6 17	Duncannon ....·	1 14	5 09	12 14
Summerhill....	7 22	11 56	6 22	Cove	1 22	5 17	12 22
Wilmore........	7 30	12 03	6 30	N. C. Crossing	1 27	5 22	12 27
Portage.........	7 38	12 09	6 38	Sid.W.of b'dge	1 30	5 25	12 30
Lillys...........	7 49	12 19	6 49	Rockville S'ch	1 35	5 30	12 35
Cresson.........	7 58	12 27	6 58	Harrisburg.....	1 45	5 45	1 00
Gallitzia........	8 07	12 35	7 07	Highspire	2 15	5 58	1 13
Kittanning Pt.	8 26	12 55	7 26	Middletown....	2 25	6 05	1 21

[CONTINUE   PAGE 5.]

(6)

PENNSYLVANIA CENTRAL RAILROAD, (CONTINUED.)

Trains going West leave Stations as follows:

	Balt. Exp. A.M.	Phila. Exp. A.M.	Fast Line. P.M.	Mail. P.M.		Balt. Exp. A.M.	Phila. Exp. A.M.	Fast Line. P.M.	Mail. P.M.
Mineral Point	8 38	9 17	9 46	8 42	George's.........	10 34	11 11	11 34	10 47
Cross'g Switch	8 46	9 25	9 53	8 50	Greensburg ...	10 42	11 18	11 42	10 57
Conemaugh ...	8 51	9 30	9 58	8 55	Radebaugh's..	10 47	11 23	11 47	11 03
Johnstown	8 57	9 36	10 04	9 01	Penn Station..	10 55	11 30	11 54	11 13
Cambria Sid'g	9 02	9 41	10 09	9 06	Manor..........	10 58	11 33	11 58	11 19
Slackwater S.	9 11	9 49	10 17	9 15	Irwin's..........	11 04	11 38	12 02	11 25
Nineveh.........	9 19	9 57	10 25	9 25	Stewart's	11 14	11 47	12 13	11 37
New Florence.	9 28	10 08			Walls...........	11 19	11 52	12 18	11 43
Lockport.......	9 38	10 16			Turtle Creek..	11 22	11 55	12 21	11 47
Bolivar	9 41	10 19			Brinton's........	11 25	11 57	12 24	11 50
Blairsville Br.	9 52	10 23		00	Wilkinsburg...	11 36	12 07	12 35	12 03
Hillside.........	10 00	10 37	11 02	10 09	East Liberty...	11 41	12 12	12 40	12 09
Derry............	10 07	10 45	11 09	10 18	Outer Station.	11 50	12 20	12 50	12 20
Latrobe.........	10 19	10 56	11 20	10 31	PITTSBURG..	12 00	12 30	1 00	12 30
Beatty's.........	10 25	11 02	11 25	10 37					

Accommodation Trains Pennsylvania Rail Road.

PHILADELPHIA DIVISION.

PARKESBURG ACCOMMODATION
   Leaves West Philadelphia at 5:50 P. M., arriving at Parkesburg 8:10 P. M.
   Leaves Parkesburg at 7:00 A. M., arriving at Philadelphia 9:45 A. M.

LANCASTER TRAIN
   Leaves Philadelphia at 4:00 P. M., arriving at Columbia at 8:20 P. M.
   Leaves Columbia at 8:15 A. M., arrives at Philadelphia 12:50 P. M.

HARRISBURG ACCOMMODATION
   Leaves Philadelphia at 2:30 P. M., arrives at Harrisburg 8:00 P. M.
   Leaves Harrisburg 4:00 P. M., arrives at Philadelphia 9.55 P. M.

MOUNT JOY ACCOMMODATION
   Leaves Lancaster at 11:05 A. M. and 7:50 P. M., arrives at Harrisburg
   12:55 P. M and 4:40 P. M.
   Leaves Harrisburg 7:00 A. M. and 4:10 P. M., arrives at Lancaster 8:40
   A. M. and 5:48 P. M.

WEST CHESTER TRAINS
   Leave Philadelphia at 8:45 A. M., 12:30 and 4:00 P. M.
   Arrive at West Chester 10:30 A. M., 2:30 and 6:00 P. M.
   Returning, leave West Chester at 6:20 and 10:50 A. M. and 3:45 P. M., arrive
   at Philadelphia 8:25 A. M , 12:50 and 5:25 P. M.

(CONTINUED ON PAGE 5.)

PENNSYLVANIA CENTRAL RAILROAD, (CONTINUED.)

Trains going East leave Stations as follows:

	Express A. M.	Fast A. M.	Mail P. M.		Express A. M.	Fast A. M.	Mail P. M.
Branch Inter...	2 28	6 08	1 23	Parkesburg....	4 28	8 20	3 20
Conewago Sid	2 38	6 18	1 33	Chandler's.....	4 32	8 23	3 23
Elizabethtown	2 42	6 28	1 43	Coatesville.....	4 39	8 30	3 31
Kuhnz's Sidi'g	2 58	6 36	1 51	Gallagherville	4 51	8 40	3 42
Mount Joy......	3 04	6 44	1 58	Downingtown.	4 56	8 45	3 47
Landisville.....	3 13	6 53	2 08	Oakland........	5 06	8 55	3 56
Dillerville......	3 27	7 07	2 21	Steamboat.....	5 13	9 02	4 03
Lancaster,.....	3 30	7 25	2 25	W'stch'st'r Int	5 22	9 09	4 12
Bird-in-Hand .	3 46	7 40	2 40	Paoli............	5 26	9 12	4 16
Gordonville...	3 54	7 47	2 47	Ea▉▉........	5 36	9 22	4 26
Leaman Place.	3 58	7 52	2 51	M▉▉Cor...	5 45	9 28	4 33
Kinzer's.........	4 05	7 58	2 58	W▉e Hall....	5 50	9 35	4 40
Gap.............	4 12	8 04	3 04	City Avenue...	6 00	9 45	4 50
Christiana......	4 18	8 10	3 09	W. Philadel'ia	6 10	9 55	5 00
Penningtonv'e	4 21	8 14	3 13	PHILAD'A	6 20	10 05	5 10

Accommodation Trains Pennsylvania Railroad, (CONTINUED.)

WESTERN ACCOMMODATION TRAIN AND FAST "EMIGRANT LINE," Leaves the Depot, No. 137 Dock Street, Philadelphia, every afternoon (except Sunday) at 5 o'clock.

This line affords accommodation to Emigrants and Families moving West, who seek a CHEAP and COMFORTABLE, and at the same time "*expeditious*" passage for themselves and household goods. Through Tickets are sold to all prominent places in the West, South-West and North-West, at about half first class fare.　　　　　FRANCIS FUNK, Agent.

WESTERN DIVISION.

JOHNSTOWN ACCOMMODATION
　Leaves Pittsburgh at 2:55 P. M., arrives at Johnstown, 7:18 P. M.
　Leaves Johnstown, 6:05 A. M., arrives at Pittsburgh, 10,15 A. M.
FIRST TRAIN TO WALL'S STATION
　Leaves Pittsburgh at 6:40 A. M., arrives at Wall's, 7:39 A. M.
　Leaves Wall's, 5:40, arrives at Pittsburgh, 6:40 A. M.
SECOND TRAIN TO WALL'S STATION
　Leaves Pittsburgh at 11:40 A. M., arrives at Wall's, 12:46 P. M.
　Leaves Wall's 7:40 A. M., arrives at Pittsburgh, 8:45 A. M.
THIRD TRAIN TO WALL'S STATION
　Leaves Pittsburgh at 4:20 P. M., arrives at Wall's, 4:50 P. M.
　Leaves Wall's 12:50 P. M., arrives Pittsburgh, 2:00 P. M.
FOURTH TRAIN TO WALL'S STATION
　Leaves Pittsburgh at 6:20 P. M., arrives at Wall's, 7,10 P. M.
　Leaves Wall's, 5:15 P. M., arrives at Pittsburgh at 6:00 P. M.

A FEW LAW AND OTHER POINTS APPLYING TO RAILROAD TRAVEL.

The law that governs the relation of Railroad Companies to the public as common carriers, is so imperfectly understood, that honest meaning men are often led into litigation, who have not had the least ground on which to sustain an honest claim, for damages caused by the company or its agents. Some leading points are therefore given, as proper in a publication of this character.

RIGHTS OF THE RAILROAD COMPANY.

The right to make and enforce rules for its own protection, among which the regulations as to the conduct of passengers; such rules must not conflict with common law or special enactments.

A company cannot be held for damages resulting from passengers standing upon the platforms, or the putting of any portion of the body out of the windows; such conduct being against the rules of all Railroad Companies.

A company cannot be held for any accident resulting from an attempt to get on or off a car while in motion. If, however, passengers should leap from a car under the influence of a well founded fear of collision, the Company is liable; but again, if a passenger, being carried past the station where he desired to stop jumps off without waiting for the train to stop; he does so at his own risk, the company not being liable for his imprudence, for "If a passenger is negligently carried beyond the station where he intended to stop, and had a right to be let off, he can recover compensation for the inconvenience, because these are direct consequences of the wrong done him."

A Company cannot be held for any accident to a passenger riding upon the baggage car, locomotive, or tender, even at the invitation of a person, (except the conductor) engaged in running the train, such passenger not being in his proper place. An individual riding free upon an engine, baggage car, freight or passenger train, by invitation of any of the persons working the train, except the conductor, cannot recover from the Company for injuries he may sustain; train hands having no right to permit any one to ride on any part of the train, either free or for pay.

If a company chooses to carry passengers for a specified time at a reduced rate, as during excursions, the tickets being good only for a certain number of days, or until a certain time; passengers are required to conform to that time, and tickets presented afterwards can be lawfully refused, as the contract has not been conformed to on the part of the passenger. Such excursion tickets are not legally transferable to any other person.

WHEN RAILROAD COMPANIES ARE LIABLE FOR LOSS OF LIFE OR INJURY TO PERSON.

1st. If caused by a collision with any train, or any obstacle placed upon the road by the Company's agents, or left there by their negligence. If, however, a collision occurred from a vehicle crossing the road, the engineer having given fair warning at the distance regulated by law and custom, action for damages will not hold, nor can recovery be had where the accident is caused by cattle straying upon the road, or from obstructions placed upon the track by malicious persons.

2d. If death or injury is caused by the breaking of a bridge, and it is in proof and clearly established that the timbers of the bridge have been tampered with, or removed by malicious persons, the Company is not liable.

3d. Where death or injury have resulted from a car running off the track, but negligence of the agents of the Company having charge of the track must be proved.

4th. If death or injury is caused by the breaking of a car axle.

5th. If death or injury is caused by the explosion of a locomotive.

6th. A Company is liable for death or injury under any circumstances where it has resulted from the negligence of the Company or its employees; but such negligence must be clearly proven.

LIABILITY FOR INJURY TO PERSONAL PROPERTY.

No damages can be claimed from a Company for destruction of cattle upon its track, where the charter of the Company or special enactments do not bind it to fence its track. The track is the exclusive property of the Company, and cattle found thereon may be taken up as estrays.

All the baggage entrusted to the Company's agents must, if lost, be paid for by the Company; but it is incumbent upon the passenger to use all due diligence in getting and retaining proper proofs of its delivery; and where a Company gives *checks* for the baggage entrusted to its agents, the passenger must attend to getting his baggage checked and retain the duplicate checks. If he lose the duplicate check, and it is found and presented by another party, who gets the baggage, an action will not lie against the Company *for the wrong delivery.* A reasonable time must, however, be given to the Company to make search for such lost baggage. The owner of the baggage is a competent witness to prove its contents.

It is against the rules of all Companies to take baggage into passenger cars although it is done constantly by sufferance. Such baggage is at the risk of its owner.

Companies are not liable for valuable trunks of jewelry, money, or merchandise, unless special terms are made by the owner with the Company, or its agent; the liabilities of Companies for lost baggage being simply for such wearing apparel, books, and other articles as are necessary for the journey.

Railroad Companies are not obliged to make any exertion to recover any article of baggage, taken into a passenger car, nor liable for it if lost or stolen, such action of a traveler being contrary to the rules of all Railroads.

A Company is liable for damage to baggage resulting from careless handling, on the plea of gross negligence on the part of the Company's servants.

RIGHTS AND DUTIES OF THOSE WORKING A TRAIN.

A conductor of a train has absolute control over it, and is the superior officer of all engaged in working the train.

A conductor has a right to demand a sight of his ticket from any passenger as often as he chooses to ask it.

A Conductor has the right to put any passenger off a train for drunkenness, obscenity, or acting in any disorderly manner, whether such individual has paid his fare or not.

A Conductor has a right to put off a train any individual who trespasses any rule laid down for the safety of the passengers, or the protection of the Company, such as standing upon the platform, interfering with the bell ropes or car brakes, etc.

Where passengers are put off cars for violation of rules, or for other causes, justifiable in law and railroad usage, care must be taken that the cars have stopped, otherwise a Company is liable, if damages result to the person ejected, from the motion of the cars.

A Company has also a right to discriminate between those who pay their passage on the cars, or purchase tickets at the Company's office, and a conductor may eject from the cars any individual who, in paying his passage on the cars, resists the payment of such additional charge per mile, as a Company may have seen proper to impose in such cases.

A Conductor has the right of placing passengers for different points, in such cars as will most facilitate his collection of fares and tickets.

A Conductor has no right to deprive a man of a seat which he has taken, and it is presumed paid for, not even for the accommodation of a lady.

A Conductor has no right to take a passenger whom he cannot furnish with a seat, unless the passenger, having been informed of the fact, is willing to take his chance.

The duty of the brakeman is to attend to the brake, and he should not be importuned with questions.

The place of duty of the baggage master is the baggage car. He has no right to give out a piece of checked baggage unless the duplicate check is presented, even if he knows that such baggage is the property of the person applying for it. He must handle all baggage with ordinary care, or the Company is liable for damages for carelessness.

TICKETS.

Always purchase tickets at the office before entering the car. You will save trouble and the additional fare charged on most roads. It has been decided that where a ticket is sold, good for a specified time, at a rate lower than that charged for those permanently good, the reduction in fare is a valid legal consideration, and the ticket cannot be used after the time expires.

A case was decided by Judge R. P. Marion, of the 8th District, Cattaraugus Circuit, New York, in which the ticket was "Good for three days," and "for a continuous trip only," in which the party got off—waited for another train, seven days after, was charged fare, refused to pay and was ejected. Action for assault and battery was non-suited, because of special terms of contract. Passengers who lose or mislay their tickets, can be made to pay a second time—decided in a case before Judge Foote. Children between four and twelve years, are usually charged half price.

Pennsylvania Rail Road Company.

————o————

J. EDGAR THOMSON,	President,	Philadelphia.
THOS. A. SCOTT,	Vice President,	"
EDMUND SMITH,	Secretary,	"
THOS. T. FIRTH,	Treasurer,	"
HERMAN J. LOMBAERT,	Controller & Aud'r,	"
ENOCH LEWIS,	Gen'l Sup't,	Altoona.
GEO. C. FRANCISCUS,	Sup't Phil. Div.,	Philadelphia.
SAM. D. YOUNG,	" East. "	Harrisburg.
ROBT. PITCAIRNS,	" Middle "	Altoona.
ANDREW CARNEGIE,	" West. "	Pittsburgh.
WM. H. WILSON,	Chief Engineer,	Altoona.
LEWIS L. HOUPT,	Gen'l Ticket Agt.	Philadelphia.
H. H. HOUSTON,	Gen'l Freight Agt.	"

THE PENNSYLVANIA CENTRAL R. R.

This road having its eastern terminus at Philadelphia, is justly to be considered one of, and perhaps *the* best road in the United States. From Philadelphia to Pittsburgh the road runs a distance of 356 miles, of which 291 miles are double track. The entire road is constructed in the most admirable manner, and the firmness of its bed, the solidity and evenness of its track, do not fail to call forth the encomiums of travelers; so forcibly does the smooth and comparatively quiet running of its cars, contrast with the wearying tormenting motion of cars on so many of our American roads. The care and skill with which its trains are run, is evidenced by the fact, that out of 3,000,000 passengers carried during the last three years, none have lost their lives from accidents, the result of negligence of the Compa- or its agents.

The first survey for a railroad was made in 1838. In 1841 the Board of Canal Commissioners appointed an engineer to make a full survey for a railway from Harrisburg to Pittsburgh. In 1845 the first meeting of the citizens of Philadelphia was held, in relation to building the road. In 1846 a law was obtained to incorporate the Pennsylvania Railroad Company. A town meeting of the citizens of Philadelphia was called as soon as the Act was passed, and a committee appointed to prepare an address to the citizens, urging the measure. The address met with a warm response; private and corporate subscriptions were soon obtained, and there was no longer any doubt of the success of the road left. The process of constructing the road; was commenced under S. V. Merrick, President, Geo. V. Bacon, Treasurer, and J. Edgar Thomson, Chief Engineer, and pushed forward with great vigor and genius, to the present day; giving to the public a road unsurpassed in this country, and which, when its double track is completed its entire distance, will be without doubt the finest railway in the world.

The cost of the road, including the main line of pu) *l*.o works, is about $30,000,000; but enormous as the sum may seem it is estimated that when its double track is completed, that the *tonnage* of the road can be increased, if necessary, to one million tor.s per annum, independent of the passenger business, and the income at low rates to $5,000,000. Upon the gigantic proportions, which the business of this road must in the future assume, we have no space to theorize, and proceed to make such mention of its various Stations, as is necessary.

Philadelphia.

New York trains leave at 1.30, 6.00, 8,00 and 11.00, A. M., and 2.00, 3.00, 4.00, 6.15, 11.15, P. M.

For Accommodation Trains of Penna. Central Rail Road, see pages 4 and 5.

For Regular Trains of Pennsylvania Central Rail Road, see pages 2 and 3.

The City of Philadelphia, the Eastern terminus of the Pennsylvania Railroad, is second in importance to no city in the United States. The entire length of the city, as now consolidated, is twenty-three miles, and the average breadth five miles. The densely inhabited portion of this area is about four miles on the Delaware and two and a half miles on the Schuylkill, having a breadth between the two rivers of 12.098 feet. The population is estimated at over 600,000, and the number of dwellings, shops and manufactories are estimated at 100,000. There are 7,400 stores, 299 churches, 304 public school houses, 18 banks, 11 market houses, 8 medical schools, 7 gas works, 5 water works, 15 public halls, 350 miles cobble pavements, 500 miles of foot pavements, 5,631 gas and fluid lamps, 9 public squares, 14 cemeteries, 9 railroad depots, and 90 fire engine houses.

Any mention, however brief, of all the branches of the vast and multiform business transacted in so large a city, is, of course, not to be attempted in a publication of such limited space as this. A brief digest of the facts in relation to the more leading pursuits of her business population is all that can be attempted.

Reaching by railroad and canal vast and inexhaustible fields of anthracite coal, within easy distance, Philadelphia is the chief seat of the anthracite coal trade, and her receipts of the mineral are about 3,500,000 tons annually. The wharves of the Reading Railroad, one of the principal places of the shipment of coal, are in themselves a curiosity worthy of the notice of strangers. For locomotives Philadelphia is justly renowned, and those manufactured there are to be seen on every railroad in the United States. One of the largest of the establishments for the manufacture of locomotives, when fully occupied, employs 1,400 hands, and has turned out three complete locomotives in a week. In the making of iron Philadelphia is a prominent point, and there is a large amount of capital employed in the various establishments within the limits of the city. Among other establishments working in iron there are 10 rolling mills, employing 700 hands, producing 17,070 tons of rolled iron annually. There are 5 foundries devoted to the manufacture of stoves, producing about 25,000 tons yearly; 3 foundries occupied with casting hollow ware; 6 foundries occupied in casting iron fronts for buildings. There are also a large number of extensive establishments engaged in the manufacture of the various descriptions of machinery, also several manufacturing gas and water works aparatus. Hardware, such as saws, shovels, forks, locks, bolts, edged tools and cutlery are also largely produced.

It is estimated that the entire iron manufacture of Philadelphia, embracing the rolling mills, foundries, locomotive works, machine shops, railroad car factories, and all the smaller branches, give employment to over 10,000 hands, and annually produce articles to the value of $12,852, 150. As a manufacturing point for textile fabrics, Philadelphia is very conspicuous, there being in the city and immediate vicinity 9,569 power looms, and 282,297 spindles running on cotton, wool and silk, employing 13,557 hands, and producing goods to the value of $17,140,050. The entire value of the branches of productive or manufacturing industry are summed up in "Philadelphia and her Manufactures " at $132,348,488.

As a dry goods market, some idea of its extent may be formed by the figures given in the report of the Philadelphia Board of Trade for 1860, which estimates that $73,500,000 of dry goods are annually distributed from that city to other markets, and the number of jobbing houses set down at 259.

Hestonville, Philadelphia 4 miles; Pittsburgh 352 miles.
Flag Station. Only Accommodation Trains stop.

A small village formed by the residences of persons doing business in Philadelphia, It contains about 300 inhabitants.

City Avenue, Philadelphia 6 miles; Pittsburgh 350 miles.
Flag Station for Accommodation Trains only.

Merion. Philadelphia 7 miles; Pittsburgh 349 miles.
Flag Station for Accommodation Trains only.

This station is situated in Merion township, Montgomery county. This district of Pennsylvania was settled by the Welsh, among whom were a large number of Friends. One of the early meeting houses of this denomination, erected in 1698, and still in use, is near this station.

Libertyville, Phila. 8 miles; Pittsburgh 348 miles.
Flag station for Accommodaton Trains only

Athensville, Philadelphia 9 miles; Pittsburgh 347 miles.
Flag station. Only Accommodation Trains stop.

A small village in Montgomery county. 200 population.

Haverford, Philadelphia, 10 miles; Pittsburgh, 346 miles.
Flag station for Mail and Accommodation Trains only.
This station is in Delaware county, and this part of the county is noted as
the birth district of the celebrated artist West.

White Hall, Philadelphia, 11 miles; Pittsburgh, 345 miles.
Flag station. Only Accommodation Trains stop.

West Haverford, Philad., 11½ miles; Pittsburgh, 344½ miles.
Flag station. Mail and Accommodation Trains only stop.

Villa Nova, Philadelphia, 12 miles; Pittsburgh, 344 miles.
Accommodation Trains only stop.
A Roman Catholic College is situated here.

Morgan's Corner, Philad., 14 miles; Pittsburgh, 342 miles
Mail and Accommodation Trains stop regularly.

Eagle, Philadelphia, 17 miles, Pittsburgh, 339 miles.
Mail on time, going West, stops.
This station is in Delaware county. One and a-half miles south of this
station is an ancient Welsh church, erected in 1717. In the burial ground
attached are interred the remains of Gen. Anthony Wayne.

Almira, Philadelphia, 18 miles; Pittsburgh, 338 miles.
Flag station for Accommodation Trains only.

Reeseville, Philadelphia, 19 miles; Pittsburgh, 337 miles.
Flag station for Accommodation Trains only.

Paoli, Philadelphia, 21 miles; Pittsburgh, 335 miles.
Mail and Accommodation Trains only stop.
About two miles south of this station is the locality of the action between
the British and American troops, on the night of September 20th, 1777, com-
monly known as the Paoli massacre. The Americans, numbering 1,500, under
the command of Gen. Wayne, were surprised by a large force of British, under Gen. Gray. After a short struggle, the Americans, overwhelmed by superior numbers, retreated. One hundred and fifty Americans were killed and
wounded; many were massacred, after all resistance had ceased. The neighborhood of this station is replete with memorials of the revolution. A few
miles to the right is Valley Forge, which, although not strictly on the line
of the railroad, is near enough to class as one of the historical interests of
the route.

Green Tree, Philadelphia, 22 miles; Pittsburgh, 334 miles-
Flag station. Mail and Accommodation Trains only stop.
Gen. Anthony Wayne, in his lifetime, resided in this vicinity. Born in
Easton township, Montgomery county, Jan. 1, 1745, he entered the army in
1775 as colonel of a corps of volunteers. At the peace of 1783, he returned

to private life. In 1789 he was a member of the Pennsylvania Convention. In 1792 he succeeded Gens. Harmar and St. Clair in the command of the North-Western frontier. His life of peril and of glory ended in 1796, at Presque Isle, by his death in a cabin of that outpost. His remains were interred, by his own request, at the foot of the flag-staff of the fort, from whence they were removed, in 1809, by his son, Col. Isaac Wayne, and re-nterred in Radnor churchyard, as previously mentioned.

West Chester, Intersection. Philad. 23 miles; Pitts. 333 miles.
Mail, on time, going West stops; East, stops.

Junction of a branch to West Chester, 9 miles distant, the county seat of Chester county. A large, handsome village, containing many fine residences. For hours of trains, see page 4.

Garrett's Siding, Philad., 25 miles; Pittsburgh, 331 miles.
Flag station for Accommodation Trains only.

A fine view of the noted Chester Valley is obtained after leaving this station.

Steamboat, Philadelphia, 26 miles; Pittsburgh, 330 miles.
Mail, on time, going West, stops.

This station derives its name from an old hotel in the vicinity, whose sign was a painting of a steamboat.

Walkertown, Philadelphia, 29 miles; Pittsburgh, 327 miles.
Flag Station for Accommodation Trains only.

Oakland, Philadelphia, 30 miles; Pittsburgh, 326 miles.
Mail, on time, going West, stops.

This station is on the south side of Chester Valley. Between this and the next station the road crosses one of the highest and largest bridges on the route. It is composed of four spans, of 130 feet each. It was erected in 1838, and has since been rebuilt in a very substantial manner.

Downingtown, Philadelphia, 34 miles; Pittsburgh, 322 miles.
All trains stop here 4 minutes for wood and water.

At Downingtown a newly constructed Branch—the "East Brandy-wine and Waynesburg Road," extends along the margin of Brandy-wine Creek, through a fertile and beautiful valley, a distance of 18 miles.

Waynesburg Branch. Distance 18 miles.
Leave Downington 9:00. A. M. and 6:00 P. M. Arrive at Waynesburg 10:30 A. M. and 7:00 P. M.
Returning leave Waynesburg 6:30 A. M. 2:00 P. M. Arrive at Downington 7:30 A. M. 3:30 P. M., Philad'a 9:40 A. M. 5:20 P. M.

This little branch is just beginning to pour its ample store of agricultural wealth into the main channel of the Pennsylvania road, and promises to be an important means of improvement to the section of country through which it passes.

(17)

From this point the Chester Valley road diverges, traversing the valley of that name, and extending twenty-ode miles in almost a straight line to Bridgeport, on the Schuylkill, 16 miles from Philadelphia, where it connects with the Philadelphia and Norristown and Norristown and Reading roads.

Downingtown is a quiet country village, originally settled by emigrants from Birmingham, England. · At this point the road crosses the north branch of the Brandywine, on the banks of which, at Chadd's ford, fifteen miles below this station, was fought the battle of Brandywine, between the English and American forces, on the 11th of Sept., 1777; Lord Cornwallis commanding the British, and Washington the Americans.

Gallagherville, Philad., 35 miles; Pittsburgh, 321 miles.
Flag Station for Accommodation Trains only.

Caln, Philadelphia, 38 miles; Pittsburgh, 318 miles.
Flag Station; Only Accommodation Trains stop.

Coatesville, Philadelphia, 39 miles; Pittsburgh, 317 miles.
Flag station. Mail and Accommodation Trains stop.
Settled in 1725, by Lindsay Coats; population now, 600. The town is laid out on the banks of the west branch of the Brandywine, across which the road passes, over a bridge 75 feet high and 850 long.

Midway, Philadelphia, 40 miles; Pittsburgh, 316 miles.
Flag station. Accommodation Trains stop.
Station derives its name from being the old midway point between Philadelphia and Columbia.

Chandlers, Philadelphia, 44 miles; Pittsburgh, 312 miles.
A Flag station. Mail and Accommodation Trains only stop.

Parkesburg, Philadelphia, 45 miles; Pittsburgh, 311 miles.
Parkesburg Accommodation Train leaves for Philadelphia at 6.20 A. M.; arrives there 9.10, A. M.
A village of about 500 inhabitants. The settlement was commenced about the year 1832. The repair shops for the Philadelphia division of the road are located here.

Penningtonville, Philad'a, 49 miles; Pittsburgh, 307 miles.
Flag station. Mail and Accommodation Trains stop when signaled, or when passengers desire to get off.
This is the last station in Chester county. The village is situated on Octoraro creek. Population, 400.

Christiana, Philadelphia, 50 miles; Pittsburgh, 306 miles.
· Flag station. Mail and Accommodation Trains only stop.
The village contains about 300 population, and is situated at the head of Chester Valley, just over Chester county line, in Lancaster county. The

town is somewhat noted as the scene of a riot in 1851, occasioned by the attempt of some Marylanders to arrest some runaway slaves.

Lancaster county, into which the traveler west enters at Christiana station, is one of the most noted of the interior counties of Pennsylvania. As the birth-place of Robert Fulton, it will hardly fail to awaken an intesest in the traveler who journeys over its surface by aid of the power which his genius made practically useful. As the residence of James Buchanan, ex-President of the United States, it possesses a political interest. John C. Calhoun came near being born in its borders, his parents, who were Scotch-Irish, having removed from this county to South Carolina a *very* short time before his birth.

Gap. Philadelphia, 52 miles; Pittsburgh, 304 miles.
Flag Station; Mail and Accommodation Trains only stop.
So called from its locality at the mouth of a gap through the Mine Ridge.

Kinzers, Philadelphia 55 miles; Pittsburgh, 301 miles.
Flag Station; Mail and Accommodation Trains only stop

Leaman Place, Philadelphia, 59 miles; Pittsburgh, 297 miles.
All trains stop 4 minutes for wood and water.
Junction of a branch railway to Strasburg, an early German settlement, 3 miles distant, containing about 1000 inhabitants.

Pequa-creek, whose main channel is crossed by the road west of this depot, was a favorite locality of the Shawnee Indians, who had a village called by the same name at its mouth. These Shawnees were the remnants of a tribe who migrated from South Carolina about the latter part of 1600—Conygham says 1678; Bancroft, 1698. The early part of the century, 1600—1700, the interior of Pennsylvania was a desolate wilderness, as may be judged from the fact that in 1792, the number of Indian fighting men in Pennsylvania being computed, there were only 700, one-half of whom were the Shawnees, already mentioned as migrating from South Carolina, 1678—1698. During 1600—1700 the lower valley of the Susquehanna was a vast unpopulated highway, through which the various tribes of the northern and southern latitudes were frequently passing, in hunting or predatory excursions, and in which desperate battles were fought by the various tribes. That it was a "dark and bloody ground" is evident, from the fact that nearly a century after the migration of the southern tribe, the chief of the Cayugas, in 1755, told the Moravians, who had settled at Wyalusing, that it was not a fit place, all that country having been stained with blood.

Gordonville, Philadelphia, 60 miles; Pittsburgh, 296 miles.
Flag Station. Accommodation Trains only stop.
The station is sometimes called Concord; it has a population of 200, and is a grain depot for the surrounding country.

Bird-in-Hand, Philadelphia, 63 miles; Pittsburgh, 293 miles.
Mail, on time, going West, stops; East, stops.
The true name of the town is Enterprise. The origin of its railroad name obscure. After leaving Bird-in-Hand, Mill Creek, a branch of the Cones-

toga, is crossed by the road. One mile east of Lancaster the road passes over Conestoga Creek.

Lancaster, Philadelphia, 70 miles; Pittsburgh, 286 miles.

All trains stop at this station.

Lancaster Accommodation, which leaves Philadelphia at 4:00, P. M., arrives here at 7:44, P. M. Same train leaves Lancaster 9:00, A. M.; arrives at Philadelphia 12:50.

The fourth city of the state of Pennsylvania. Laid out in 1700, by Andrew Hamilton, it was in June, 1797, incorporated as a Borough, and as a city, in 1818. From 1799 to 1812, the town was the seat of government of the state. Many incidents of interest are connected with the history of this locality. In 1777, while Philadelphia was held by the British, Congress, for a short time, assembled here. In 1763, occurred in the town, the massacre of the Conestoga Indians, by the "Paxton Boys." On the night of Dec. 14, of that year, a number of armed men, on horseback, made a descent upon the Indian village, most of the men were absent. Those remaining, and the women and children were butchered, and the village burnt. The authorities hastily collected the scattered remnants of the tribe, into a stone work-house, in the town of Lancaster; but on Sunday, the 27th, while the inhabitants were at church, the Paxton Boys rode into town, forced the doors of the work-house, and murdered the fourteen Indians therein contained. The pretext for the massacre was that the feeble remnant of the Conestogas, were said to be harboring two or three hostile Indians. The affair created, in its day, great excitement. The Paxton Boys threatened to visit Philadelphia, and destroy some Moravian Indians, who had fled to that city for shelter.— The people of the city were much alarmed, and several companies were formed to repel the attack. The "Paxton Boys" learning, upon their approach to the Schuylkill, the reception prepared for them, retreated to their homes. The Paxton Boys were from the Townships of Donegal and Paxton, largely settled by Scotch-Irish.

The present city of Lancaster is substantially built. The streets are laid off at right angles, and lighted with gas. It contains a population of about 17,000. There are 18 churches in the city. Its court house, costing $100,-000, is a fine building. The new Penitentiary, seen on the left, going west, is a well arranged structure, costing $110,000. Quite a number of industrial works are established here, and ten McAdamized roads radiate to different sections of the country.

Dillerville, Philadelphia, 71 miles; Pittsburgh, 285 miles.

Flag station. Mail and Accommodation Trains only stop. Here the branch road takes off to Columbia and to Middletown, connecting at Columbia with trains to Little York and Baltimore. This branch road strikes the Susquehanna near Columbia, and follows it by easy grades to Middletown, where it again joins the main line. This route is used for the heavy freight trains from and to the West. Two Passenger Trains run each way.

Landisville, Philadelphia, 78 miles; Pittsburgh, 278 miles.
Mail, on time, going West, stops; East, stops.

Beyond this station the road crosses the little Conestoga, and approaches the Conewago Hills.

This station is on the ridge dividing the valleys of the Little Conestoga and Big Chiquesalunga creek. West of the station a bridge 300 feet long, is crossed over which the road passes Big Chiquesalunga creek, soon after we arrive at Little Chiquesalunga

Mount Joy, Philadelphia, 82 miles; Pittsburgh, 274 miles.
All trains stop at this station.

The town was settled in 1812, by emigrants from Ireland, by whom it was named after Mount Joy, in the North of Ireland. The town was incorporated as a borough in 1831. A cave in the neighborhood, is said to be an interesting and curious object to visit. The borough contains a population of 1800, and has five churches. Several manufactories give life and bustle to the town.

RICHLAND, a small village, properly a portion of Mount Joy

Elizabethtown, Philadelphia, 89 miles; Pittsburgh, 267 miles.
All trains stop at this station.

Before reaching this point, the road passes through a tunnel, 900 feet long, 15 feet wide, and 15 feet high. It cost $100,000. From the vicinity of Elizabethtown, westward, the road traverses the Conwago Hills, and crosses the Conewago creek, by a bridge 450 feet long, and 85 feet high. After crossing the Canewago, the road enters Dauphin County, which was separated from Lancaster County, in 1785. Dauphin County has a length of 33 miles, a breadth of 16 miles, and an area of 533 square miles. The mountain regions abound in anthracite coal. Lindley Murray, the celebrated author of "the English Grammar," and William Darby, the eminent geographer, are among the noted men who claim birth-right in the county.

Middletown, Philadelphia, 97 miles; Pitttsburgh, 259 miles.
All trains stop at this station.

Located at the mouth of Swatara Creek, on the Susquehanna River. The town derives its name from having been, in Turnpike days, half way between Carlisle and Lancaster. It was laid out in 1755, by Geo. Fisher. The population of the town is now about 3000. Middletown is an important lumber depot. A large business in coal, is also transacted here. There are two iron furnaces, a foundery, and several flouring and saw mills in the town

Highspire, Philadelphia, 101 miles; Pittsburgh, 255 miles.
Mail, on time, going West, stops; East, stops.

Laid out about 40 years ago ; population 600. On the opposite side of the river commences the York Hills, and the South Mountain.

Harrisburg, Philadelphia, 107 miles; Pittsburgh, 249 miles.
Express, on time, going West, stops 8 m; East, 10 m.
Express, on time, going West, stops 8 m; East, 10 m.
Mail, both East and West, stops 20 minutes for dinner.

Fast, on time, going West, stops 5 m; East, 5 m.

Mount Joy Accommodation leaves Harrisburg 7:00, A. M. and 4:10 P. M. Arrives at Lancaster, 8:40, A. M. 5:48 P. M. Returning, leaves Lancaster, 11:05 A. M., and 7:50 P. M.; arriving at Harrisburg at 12:55 P. M. and 9:40 P. M.

As the capital of the state of Pennsylvania, the interest of the tourist is naturally awakened, and we subjoin some few words, embracing some of the information that may be desired. The town was laid out in 1785, by John Harris, jr., and was incorporated as a borough in 1808. The borough is situated in Dauphin county, on the left bank of the Susquehanna, a short distance above Paxton creek. The town contains seventeen churches, two rolling mills, several founderies, one extensive car factory, the "Novelty" and the "Eagle" Works, a cotton mill, and various other similar establishments. Two daily, and four weekly papers, are published in the town.— There are the usual state and county public buildings. The Speaker's chair in the House of Representatives, is the one used by John Hancock, as President of the Continental Congress. The Senate Chamber contains fine full length portraits of Washington and of Wm. Penn; also of Columbus and Vespucius. There is also a painting of an attempt by the Indians to burn John Harris, the father of the founder of the town, who settled here in 1726 ; in which year was born John Harris, jr., said to be the first white child born west of the Conewago Hills. The Governor's Chamber contains the original charter, given by Charles II, to Penn, and portraits of all the Governors of the Commonwealth. The town is supplied with water by a water-works which cost $120.000, having a reservoir with a capacity of 1.532.192 gallons. The Pennsylvania State Lunatic Asylum is located here. It has accommodations for 250 patients. The buildings are seen on a fine bluff on the right as the traveler leaves the town going West.

Cumberland Valley Road.

1st train leaves HARRISBURG at 8:05, A. M. Arrives at CHAMBERSBURG, 11.00, A. M., Hagerstown, 12:35, P. M., 2d train leaves HARRISBURG, 1:35, P. M. Arrives at Chambersburg 4:30, P. M., Hagerstown, 6:10, P. M. Returning, 1st train leaves Hagerstown, 7:00, A. M. CHAMBERSBURG, 8:30, A. M. Arrives at HARRISBURG at 11:15, A. M. Returning, 2d train leaves Chambersburg 12:55, P. M. Arrives at Harrisburg, 3:40, P. M. Trains leaves Hagerstown at 2:45 P. M. Arrives at Chambersburg at 4:20 P. M

Northern Central Railway.

HARRISBURG TO WILLIAMSPORT.—1st train leaves Harrisburg at 3:00, Sunbury 5:43, Williamsport, 7:35, Lock Haven. 9:05, A. M. 2d Train leaves Harrisburg, 11:15, P. M. Sunbury 4:10 P. M. Williamsport, 6.10 P. M., Lock Haven 7:20 P. M

RETURNING; WILLIAMSPORT TO HARRISBURG.- -[st train leaves
Lock Haven 6.35, A. M. Williamsport, 8.15, A .M., Sunbury, 10 05,
P. M., Harrisburg, 12.45, P. M.   2d train leaves Lockhaven,
P. M., Williamsport, 9.20, P. M., Sunbury, 11.02, P. M., Harris-
burgh, 1.45, A. M.

HARRISBURG TO BALTIMORE.

Leave Harrisburg 2.00 and 6.30, A. M., 1.15, P. M.; reaching
Baltimore, 6.15, 11.30, A. M., and 5.35, P. M. RETURNING, leaves
BALTIMORE at 9.15 A. M., 2.55 and 9.15 P, M. Arrive at Harris-
burg at 1.00, 7.30 P. M., and 1.35, A. M.

COLUMBIA TO YORK.

Leave COLUMBIA, 6.15, 11.25, A. M., 1.10, and 7.00, P. M.
Returning, leave YORK 5.00, 11.40 A. M. and 4.00 P. M.

Allentown Route from New York

This route, having a distance of 182 miles, from New York to
Harrisburgh, is composed of the CENTRAL RAILROAD OF
NEW JERSEY, LEHIGH VALLEY, EAST PENNSYLVANIA
and LEBANON VALLEY RAILROADS, and has its junction
with the Pennsylvania Central at Harrisburgh. By this route

Trains from New York.					Trains to New York.			
LEAVE.	MILES.	A. M	M.	P. M.	LEAVES	A. M.	A. M.	P. M.
New York...		6.00	12.00	7.00	Harrisburg.......	2.15	8.00	2,00
			P. M,		Reading	4.14	11.15	4.20
Newark	9	6.30	12.30	7.30			P. M.	
Elizabeth	14	6.45	12.45	7.45	Allentown	5.30	12.55	5.49
Plainfield ...	26	7.12	1.21	8.13	Bethlebem........	5.45	1.07	6.07
Somerville...	38	7.38	1.50	8.40	Easton*..........	6.37	2.05†	7.00
Junction.... .	59	8.25	2.48	9.28	Junction.........	7.13	2.54	7.45
Easton........	75	9.03	3.34	10.08	Somerville	8.00	3.55	8.40
Bethlebem...	87	9.25	4.04	10.33	Plainfield..		4.25	90.9
Allentown....	92	9.38	4.20	10.43	Elizabeth.........	8.50	5.00	9.45
Reading......	128	11.07	6.00	11.57	Newark..........	9.00	5.10	9.55
		P. M.		A. M.	New York, arri.	9.35	5.50	10.30
Harris'g, ar.	183	1.15	8.20	1.55	* Breakfast.			
					† Dinner.			
					† Supper.			

Harrisburg is a great interior Railway Centre. Subjoined are tables of
Stations and distances, on Railroads radiating from Harrisburg.

Philadelphia and Erie Rail Road.

This GREAT LINE traverses the Northern and North-western Counties of Pennsylvania, to the

CITY OF ERIE, ON LAKE ERIE.

This road has been leased by the

PENNSYLVANIA RAIL ROAD COMP'Y.

And under its auspices is being rapidly opened throughout its entire length. It is now in use from

HARRISBURG TO DRIFTWOOD (2d Fork),

A distance of **177** miles on the Eastern Division, and from

SHEFFIELD TO ERIE,

A distance of **78** miles on the Western Division.

Cars run through on both trains to Lock Haven, from Philadelphia, Baltimore and Harrisburg, using the Northern Central Rail Road to Sunbury.

Magnificent Sleeping Cars attached to all Night Trains.

FIRST TRAIN LEAVES:

Philadelphia at	7:30 A. M.	Arrive at Lock Haven,	7:20 P. M.
Or Baltimore	9:15 "	Williamsport for Buffalo and	
Harrisburg,	1:15 A. M.	Rochester	6:30 "
Sunbury,	4:10 "	Arrive at Elmira,	10:30 "
Williamsport for Lock Haven,	6:50 "	" Buffalo,	6:00 A. M.

SECOND TRAIN LEAVES:

Philadelphia at	10:30 P. M.	Driftwood,	12:00 M.
Or Baltimore	9:15 "	Williamsport for Buffalo and	
Harrisburg,	3:00 A. M.	Rochester	7:55 A. M.
Sunbury,	5:43 "	Arrive at Elmira,	11:50 "
Williamsport for Driftwood,	7:35 "	" Buffalo,	7:15 P. M.

RETURNING:

FIRST TRAIN LEAVES·

Buffalo,	10:55 P. M.	Sunbury	10:10 A. M
Elmira,	4:15 P. M.	Harrisburg,	1:00 P. M
Lock Haven,	6:35 "	Arrive at Philadelphia,	5:30 "
Willliamsport,	8:15 "	" Baltimore,	5:30 "

SECOND TRAIN LEAVES:

Buffalo,	10:15 A. M.	Williamsport,	9:20 P. M.
Elmira,	5:25 P. M.	Harrisburg,	2:00 A. M.
Driftwood,	4:20 "	Arrive at Philadelphia,	6:40 "
Lock Haven,	7:45 "	" Baltimore,	6:15 "

Trains from and to Elmira, Buffalo, Niagara Falls and all Western New York, connect with the above Trains both ways at Williamsport. JOS. D. POTTS, General Manager.

Northern Central Railway.

On and after January 18th, 1863, Passenger Trains will arrive and depart from Calvert Station, as follows:

TRAINS NORTHWARD LEAVE:	TRAINS SOUTHWARD ARRIVE:
Mail, Through..............................9:15 A. M.	Mail. Through.............................. 5:35 P. M.
Express, Through........................ 9:15 P. M.	Express. Through........ .... 6:15 A. M.
Harrisburg Accommodation Way......2:55 "	Harrisburg Accommodation Way...11:30 A. M.
Parkton " " .....7:20 "	Parkton " " ... 7:40 A. M.

Mail and Express Trains make close connections with Pa. Central R. R. at Harrisburg for Pittsburgh, Columbus, Cincinnati, Indianapolis, Ft. Wayne, Chicago, and all points in the Great West; and at Elmira with the New York and Erie Rail Road, for Buffalo, Dunkirk, Niagara Falls, Rochester, Syracuse, and all points in Northern. Central & Western New York. Passengers for Northern, Central and Western New York will save 10 hours time and over 200 miles travel by this route. N. B. Express at 9:00 P. M. will stop at the following points South of Harrisburg only: Goldsborough, York, Hanover Junction, Glenrock, Parkton, Shrewsbury. Express at 9:00 P. M. connect at Harrisburg with Trains for New York City, direct, via Allentown. The Train leaving Calvert Station at 2:55 P. M will stop at all Stations. The only Train leaving on Sundays is the Express at 9:05 P. M. The only Trains arriving on Sundays are the Harrisburg Accommodation at 11:30 A. M., and the Express at 6:15 A. M. Omnibusses await the arrival of Trains from Washington, to convey Passengers to the Depot of the Northern Central Railway, Calvert Station, Baltimore. Through Tickets to all Points reached by their Line, may be obtained at the Office of the Great Penna. Route, cor. Pennsylvania Avenue and 6th St., Washington, D. C., near National Hotel, and at Calvert Station, Baltimore. ED. S. YOUNG, General Passenger Agent.
E. O. NORTON, Ticket Agent, cor. Penna. Avenue and 6th St., Washington, D. C.

Rockville. Philadelphia, 112 miles; Pittsburgh, 243 miles.
Mail Train only stops at this station.

At this point the traveler enters upon a railroad bridge across the Susquehanna. 3679 feet long.

Marysville, Philadelphia, 115 miles; Pittsburgh, 240 miles.
All trains stop at this station.

At this point the railroad crosses the track of the Northern Central road, which crosses the river by a handsome bridge, of the McCallum pattern.

Cove, Philadelphia, 117 miles; Pittsburgh, 239 miles.
Mail, going West, stops; East, stops.

This station is in Perry county, which was separated from Cumberland county in 1720. The county lies between two very lofty and distinct ranges of mountains; the Kittatinny and the Tuscarora.

Duncannon. Philadelphia, 121 miles; Pittsburgh, 234 miles.
All trains, going West, stop; Fast Line and Mail East stop.

This station is located at the mouth of Sherman's Creek. There is a rolling mill and an extensive nailery here, which employs a number of hands.

Aqueduct, Philadelphia, 125 miles; Pittsburgh, 231 miles.
Mail, going West, stops; East, stops.

Bailey's, Philadelphia, 130 miles; Pittsburgh, 226 miles.
Mail, going West, stops; East, stops.
At this station the road is fairly within the limits of the picturesque Juniata Valley, a region of great romantic beauty, and bold scenery.

Newport, Philadelphia, 134 miles; Pittsburgh, 222 miles.
All trains stop at this station 4 minutes for wood and water.
This town, the second in importance, in Perry county, is situated at the junction of Buffalo Creek with the Juniata River, and has a population o 500. It is a place of some note as a shipping point. It was laid out 1814, by a person named Reider, after whom it was formerly called Reidersville.

Millerstown, Philadelphia, 140 miles; Pittsburgh, 216 miles.
Mail, going West, stops; East, stops.
This town was laid out some sixty years ago; but as early as 1755, a block-house was constructed at this point, by William Patterson, a bold, energetic man, who also in 1798, erected a mill here. At this point the road reaches the Tuscarora Ridge, and continues for some miles along its southern slope, when it enters the famous Tuscarora Valley, situated in Juniata County.

Thompsontown, Philad., 145 miles; Pitts., 211 miles.
Mail, going West, stops; East, stops.
This town is situated in Juniata County, and was laid out about 1800.

Mexico, Philadelphia, 151 miles; Pittsburgh, 205 miles.
Mail, going West, stops; East, stops.
In 1755, before the block-house already mentioned, as constructed in that year at Millerstown, was commenced, an attempt was made to dig a cellar at a point just opposite this town. The Indians, however frustrated the effort. They came down upon the point of the little ridge overlooking the spot, and shot the workmen. A short distance above this point, is the scene of a sanguinary battle between two Indian tribes, occasioned by the quarrel of some Indian children over some grasshoppers.

Perrysville, Philadelphia, 154 miles; Pittsburgh, 202 miles.
Mail, going West, stops; East, stops.
This town stand at the junction of Tuscarora and Licking creeks, with the Juniata. It is the principal depot for the shipments of the surrounding country. It has been supposed that near the mouth of Licking creek, there was a lead mine; from the fact that, in early days, but long after the settlement of this neighborhood by whites, friendly Indians, who frequently came and encamped on Licking creek, were wont, after exhausting their supply of bullets in shooting matches, to proceed down the creek towards its mouth, and return in a short time with plenty of lead, nearly pure. The mine has never been discovered by the whites, and has been long looked upon as a myth.

Mifflin, Philadelphia, 156 miles; Pittsburgh, 200 miles.
Wood and water station; all trains stop.
Wheels at this point undergo thorough inspection.

This is the county seat of Juniata county. It was laid out in 1791, by John Harris, and named in honor of Gov. Mifflin. Much prospecting has been done for the discovery of a silver mine, supposed to be in a ridge near the town, on the railroad side of the river. An old Indian used frequently to tell of such a mine being in that locality. About ten miles from Mifflin, near to Tuscarora creek, the remains of an ancient fortification are said to be visible. After leaving this town the road follows the river course to the northwest boundary of Juniata county, where it enters Mifflin county. The road enters the latter County through a passage between Blacklog mountain on the left, and Shade mountain on the right. The scenery in this narrow gorge is of the wildest character.

Lewistown, Philadelphia, 168 miles; Pittsburgh, 188 miles.
All trains stop at this station. Stages leave this point for Bellefonte.

This town is the county seat of Mifflin county. The county was formed in 1798, and it abounds in iron ore of the best quality, from which is made the celebrated Juniata iron. There are several curious caves in the limestone districts. This county is another of the districts in this region in which it was long supposed that a lead mine was to be found. Friendly Indians, who lived in the vicinity of what is now Lewistown, frequently exhibited lead, apparently pure, which they professed to find in the neighborhood. When they went to seek it, they usually went in the direction of Granville Gap; but they would never allow any whites to accompany them. As early as 1755, Arthur Buchanan built himself a cabin where Lewistown now stands. Fort Granville, captured in 1756, by the French and Indians, was also built in 1755, near a spring, one mile above the present town. About six miles from Lewistown, on the Bellefont road, at a place now called Reedsville, was once the habitation of the famous Indian Chief, Logan. It was on the left bank of the Kishicoquilas creek, and was called Logan's Spring. Lewistown was laid out in 1790, and is on the Juniata, just above Kishicoquilas creek, which furnishes water power for a number of manufacturing establishments located in the town.

Anderson, Philadelphia, 174 miles; Pittsburgh, 182 miles.
Mail, on time, going West, stops; East, stops.

McVeytown, Philadelphia, 180 miles; Pittsburgh, 176 miles
Mail, going West, stops; East, stops.

The town is three-fourths of a mile from the station, and is situated on the canal and turnpike. It was formerly called Waynesburg. It is an incorporated bororough. Near this town is a large and curious cave, known as Henawalt's cave.

Manayunk, Philadelphia, 185 miles; Pittsburgh, 171 miles.
Mail, going West, stops; East, stops.
There is a town with a similar name, near Philadelphia.

Newton-Hamilton, Philad, 190 miles; Pitts., 166 miles.
Mail, going West, stops; East, stops.
There is near this station, a remarkable bend in the river. After a south-eastern course for several miles, it suddenly runs to the north-west, and approaches within a few hundred yards of its channel above the bend. This town was formerly known as Muhlenburg. The river at this point enters the counties of Juniata and Huntingdon. The population of the place is about 300, and the town is quite a large depot for iron and produce.

Mount-Union, Philad., 193 miles; Pittsburgh, 163 miles.
Stages run from this point to Shirleysburg, in the Augwick Valley, and Milnwood Academy, in Shade Gap.
This village is at the entrance of Jack's Mountain. After leaving Mount Union, the road runs through the midst of fine mountain scenery, which presents many sublime features. The pass through which the road is built, is known as Jack's Narrows, They are so called after a famous frontiersman, known as "Capt. Jack," whose habits invested him with a mysterious character in the eyes of the early inhabitants of these regions, which he made his stamping ground, in 1750--1755. He was known as the "Black Hunter' the "Black Rifle," the "Wild Hunter of the Juniata," the "Black Hunter of the Forest," as well as the less romantic name of "Capt. Jack." His real name was never known. He had entered the woods with a few enterprising companions, built a cabin, and cleared some land. One day, returning from hunting, he found his cabin burnt, his wife and children murdered, by the Indians. Forsaking civilized life, he lived in caves, and seizing every opportunity for revenge, he became the terror of the red man, and the protecting angel of the frontier whites. Many stories are told of his sudden and mysterious appearance, to the discomfiture and death of the Indians, and the rescue of whites from death and danger.

Mapleton, Philadelphia, 196 miles; Pittsburgh, 160 miles.
Mail, going West, stops; East, stops.

Mill Creek, Philadelphia, 200 miles; Pittsburgh, 156 miles.
Mail, going West, stops; East, stops.
On the opposite side of the river from this station, is seen Terrace mountain. Five miles from this station, we reach Huntingdon; approaching which, the character of the scenery becomes yet more marked.

Huntingdon, Philadelphia, 205 miles; Pittsburgh, 151 miles.
Wood and water Station.
All trains stop at this station.

The Huntingdon and Broad Top Railroad
Branches off at this station.

1st Train leaves Huntingdon 7:20 A. M.; arrive at Saxon 9:10; arr. at Hopewell 9.45 A. M., and Dudley 10:06 A. M.

Returning, leaves Dudley and Hopewell 10:15, A M.; Saxton 10:50 A. M., arrive at Huntingdon 12:30 P. M.

2nd Train leaves Huntingdon 3:40 P. M.; Saxton 5.20 P. M., arrive at Hopewell 5:55 P. M.

Returning, leaves Hopewell 6:40, Saxton 7:30 P. M.; reach Huntingdon 9:14 P. M.

Stages to Bedford.

This town, which rejoices in the soubriquet of "The Ancient Borough," was laid out a short time previous to the revolutionary war by the Rev. Dr. W. Smith, Provost of the University of Pennsylvania. He named the town after the Countess of Huntingdon, who had been extremely liberal in subscribing to the aid of the University, through Dr. Smith, when he was in England soliciting funds for the support of that institution. The town is the countyseat of Huntingdon county, which is rich in mineral deposits. In addition to coal and iron, lead is found in Sinking Spring Valley, and a mine in that vicinity was worked toward the close of the revolutionary war.

Petersburg, Philadelphia, 211 miles; Pittsburgh, 145 miles.
Mail, going West, stops; East, stops.

This town stands on the site of a fort that was constructed at the mouth of Shafer's creek, and where a settlement was commenced in 1770. At this point the canal and river, which have so long kept companionship with the road, part company, and sweep off to the left, while the railroad continues along the rugged course of the Little Juniata.

Barre Forge, Philadelphia, 215 miles; Pittsburgh, 141 miles.
Mail, going West, stops; East, stops.

At this point the road enters a gorge of Tuessey's mountain. Two miles above Barre the Little Juniatta makes a great bend, and the road, instead of following its course, goes through a spur of the mountain, by means of a tunnel 1,246 feet long, 20 feet wide and 16 feet high.

Spruce Creek, Philadelphia, 217 miles; Pittsburgh, 139 miles.
Stages leave this point for Northumberland County.

Spruce Creek Valley, from whence this station derives its name, contains some very extensive furnaces, whose business finds on outlet at this point.

Union Furnace, Philad., 219 miles; Pittsburgh, 137 miles.
Flag station. Mail Trains stop.

In the neighborhood of this station is Sinking Spring valley, in which was built, in 1778, Fort Robertdeau, the largest and best defended frontier post of the day. Sinking Spring Valley, as mentioned in connection with Huntingdon, is the location of the lead mines worked during the closing years of the revolutionary war. Search was made in this valley, in early days, for silver.

In 1778, when Robertdeau erected the fort at the upper lead mines, a remarkable and irregular trench, some six miles in length, and of ancient appearance, was found in the valley. It was attributed to the French, who, while they held Fort Duquesne, made extensive explorations in Ligonier Valley for the precious metals. And the trench affords ground from its great length, for belief that the search was successful. Among the curiosities of this valley are the Arch Spring and the Cave. The spring gushes from a deep hollow formed in the limestone rock, about thirty feet in breadth, with a rude arch of stone hanging over it. The water is driven out with sufficient force to drive a mill, and then sinks into the earth again, after a subterraneous course for some distance, it again emerges, and runs along the surface until it enters a large cave, which has been explored some 400 feet, to a large room, where the water falls down a chasm, and finds a passage near Canoe Mountain, emerging at its southern base.

Birmingham, Philad., 222 miles; Pittsburgh, 134 miles.

Mail train only stops at this station.

This town contains over 200 inhabitants. It had, in 1824, but nine houses, and was incorporated in 1828. Leaving this point the road still following the windings of the Little Juniatta, enters a narrow pass, having Brush mountain on the left, going west, and Eagle mountains on right.

Tyrone, Philadelphia, 225 miles; Pittsburgh, 131 miles.

TYRONE AND CLEARFIELD BRANCH.

1st Train leaves Tyrone, A. M. P. M.; arrive at Nuttall's A. M., P. M. Returning, leave Bellefonte, , A. M., P. M.; arrive at Tyrone, A. M., P. M.
2nd Train leaves Tyrone, A. M., P. M.; Bald Eagle Valley Intersection, A. M.; arrive at Bellefonte, A. M. P. M. Returning, leaves Sandy Ridge, A. M., P. M.; arrive at Tyrone A. M., P. M.

Stages leave here for Bellefonte, Jersey Shore and Williamsport.

This thriving town is situated at the mouth of Bald Eagle creek in Blair county, and has sprung up since the construction of the railroad. It contains a population of 1000. From the mouth of Bald Eagle to Altoona, the road traverses the noted Tuckahoe Valley. At this station a road branches off into Clearfield county, connecting also with the Bald Eagle Valley Road, giving an outlet to the vast resources of lumber, coal and iron for which this region is famous.

Tipton. Philadelphia, 229 miles; Pittsburgh, 127 miles.

Mail, going West, stops; East, stops.

An outlet for the Clearfield lumber district. From this point many varieties of lumber find their way to the Philadelphia and Baltimore markets.

Fostoria. Philadelphia, 230 miles; Pittsburgh, 126 miles.

Mail train only stops at this station.

So named in honor of Wm. B. Foster, a dec'd, Vice President of the road.

Bell's Mills. Philadelphia, 232 miles; Pittsburgh, 124 miles.

Express, going West, stops; East, stops.

Mail, going West, stops; East, stops.

An artesian well has been sunk here to the depth of 1200 feet, but water is not yet obtained. The pyramidical structure for boring will be seen upon the slope of the hill, to the right, going west.

Blair Furnace. Philadelphia, 236 miles; Pittsburgh, 120 miles.

Mail train only stops at this station.

In Brush mountain, near this station, is a deposit of iron ore, said to be the heaviest in Western Pennsylvania. It has been efficiently worked for more than a generation, but seems to be inexhaustible.

Altoona, Philadelphia, 239 miles; Pittsburgh, 117 miles.

Express, on time, going West, stops 20 min. for breakfast; East, stops 20 m. for tea.

Mail, on time, going West, stops 20 m. for supper; 'East, stops 15 m. for breakfast.

Fast line, on time, going West stops 1⁵ m. for tea.

At this point the **Hollidaysburg Branch** takes off.

Hollidaysburg, distant 8 miles; time, 30 minutes.

Trains leave Altoona 8:00 A. M., 10:25 A. M. and 7:15 P. M.

Hollidaysburg Trains connect with Mail east, and with Mail and Express West.

During stoppage all wheels and axles are examined and engines changed.

This town owes its formation entirely to the operations of the Pennsylvania railroad. Some few years ago its site was marked by one log hut, whose solitary inhabitant was the beginning of the population of 5000 who now inhabit this thriving borough. The office of the General Superintendent of the road is located here; also the main shops of the company, which comprises machine and car shops, iron and brass foundries, blacksmithing, painting, trimming, pattern making and tin and sheet iron shops. There are also establishments for setting up locomotives, and for making boilers and iron bridges; in fact, a heavy proportion of the equipment work of the road is done here.

The town contains four churches. The "Logan House," owned and erected by the Railroad Company, is a fine and commodiously constructed building, of fine architectural porportions. The traveler who sees it for the first time, does not fail to feel surprised that so superb a house has been erected here

Hollidaysburg Branch.

Duncansville, 6 miles from Altoona

Is 1200 feet above tide water level, and contains a population of 500. It is situated at the foot of the inclined planes of the old Portage Railroad.

Hollidaysburg, 8 miles from Altoona. Time 30 minutes.

Trains connect at Altoona with the Fast Mail East, and Express West. Trains leave for Altoona at 6:25, and 9:35, A. M., and 6:30, P. M.

This prosperous town is situated on a branch of the Big Juniata. It was laid out by one Adam Holiday, and now contains 5000 inhabitants. Its principal growth has been since 1830, at which time it had but seventy-two inhabitants. The town is well situated in the centre of a country teaming with mineral riches, and of a fine agricultural character. It is the county seat of Blair county. Several foundries and machine shops are among its business establishments. Leaving Hollidaysburg, and returning to the main route, and climb the Allegheny mountains, as we leave Altoona, at the rate of 95 feet to the mile. As the road winds up the side of the mountain a beautiful view of the magnificient scenery is obtained.

Kittanning Point, Philad., 244 miles; Pittsburgh, 112 miles.
Flag Station. Mail Trains stop.

This is a water station at the top of a heavy grade. At this point the grandest view on the whole route is presented to the sight. A vast extent of landscape is spread out before the eye, presenting all those charms of mountain scenery which enchant the lover of nature. On leaving Kittanning Point, the road soon enters the awesome darkness of the GREAT TUNNEL. This is the grand engineering triumph of the road. Its total length is 3,612 feet, its width 24 feet, its height above the rails 21½ feet. The depth below the summit of the mountain 203 feet. The tunnel was commenced October, 1851, and finished Jan. 1854, costing $540,000. During the course of its construction, three shafts were sunk to aid the tunneling. The eastern shaft was 150 feet deep, the middle 196 feet, and the western 185 feet. The sharpest curvature on the road occurs at this point; the grade is 95 feet to the mile. This horse shoe bend is one of the greatest engineering triumphs of the age.

Gallitzin, Philadelphia, 251 miles; Pittsburgh, 105 miles.
All trains stop at this station.

This station is at the western end of the great tunnel, and is in Cambria county. The line between Blair and Cambria counties, runs along the top of the ridge pierced by the great tunnel. Near the north line of the county, about one mile from the falls of the Beaver Dam and Slate Lick creek, there is said to be an ancient fortification, whose banks are four or five feet high, and overgrown with immense trees. The station was named after the Rev. Demetrius Augustine Galitzin, by birth a Russian Prince, by choice a Catholic Priest, who inspired with great love for the poor, and a desire to devote his means to charitable purposes, settled at Loretto, near this station, 1789. He died in 1840, aged 72 years, having passed the most of his life on the bleak summits of the Allegheny, in the discharge of the duties of his sacred office.

Cresson, Phila, 254 miles; Pittsburgh, 102 miles. All trains stop.

This station is named after Elliott Cresson, of Philadelphia. There is a fine hotel here, and the locality has become a popular resort during the summer months, for invalids and pleasure seekers. From this point a branch road recently constructed leads to Ebensburg, &c. Trains runs as follows:

EBENSBURG BRANCH. Distance 11 miles. Time one hour.

Leave Cresson 9:30 A. M., and 800: P. M.

Returning leave Ebensburg 6:40 A. M., and 6 35 P. M.

Lilly, Philadelphia, 257 miles; Pittsburgh, 99 miles.
Mail, on time, going West, stops. East, stops.

At the foot of Plane No. 4, on the western slope of the mountains. At this station the streams begin fairly to flow downward toward the Ohio.

Portage, Philadelphia, 261 miles; Pittsburgh, 95 miles.
Mail, going West, stops. East, stops.

This station is on the head waters of the Conemaugh River, which the railroad follows to the Blairsville Intersection.

Wilmore, Philadelphia, 264 miles; Pittsburgh, 92 miles.
Wood and water Station.
All trains stop at this station.
Stages leave this point for Ebensburgh.

A depot for the town of Jefferson, which contains about 1000 inhabitants.

Summerhill, Philadelphia, 266 miles; Pittsburgh, 90 miles.
Mail, going West, stops; East, stops.

Viaduct, Philadelphia, 270 miles; Pittsburgh, 86 miles.

At this station a fine viaduct, nearly 75 feet above the water, spans with a single arch of 80 feet, the Conemaugh. Passing through a deep cut of over a hundred feet, the road crosses an iron bridge, having an elevation of seventy-three feet.

Mineral Point, Philadelphia, 272 miles; Pittsburgh, 84 miles.
Express, going West, stops; East, stops.
Mail, going West, stops; East, stops.

Conemaugh, Philadelphia, 275 miles; Pittsburgh, 81 miles.
All trains stop at this station.

Although the grade of the road has been descending from the Great Tunnel, yet at this point its level is still 1,226 feet above tide water level.

Johnstown, Philadelphia, 277 miles; Pittsburgh, 79 miles.
All trains stop at this station.
Johnstown Accommodation leaves for Pittsburgh 6:05, A.
M. Arrives at Pittsburgh 10:15 Returning, leaves Pittsburgh 2.55 P. M. Arrives at Johnstown, 7.18 P. M.
Johnstown Accommodation stops at all regular and flag stations
when signaled. Stages leave Johnstown for Somerset.

This town occupies the site of an old Indian Village, known as Keekenapawlings-town. In the palmy days of the Pennsylvania canal, this town was an important point in canal navigation. The extensive establishment of the

Cambria Iron Works, are in the neighborhood, and are to be seen after passing across the fine iron bridge, over which the road passes, soon after leaving the Johnstown depot. The company employ 1500 operators.

Conemaugh Furnace, Philad, 285 miles; Pitts., 71 miles.
Mail, going West, stops. East, stops.

Nineveh, Philadelphia, 287 miles; Pittsburgh, 69 miles.
Wood and water Station.
Mail, on time, going West, stops.

A considerable depot for the lumber and other products of the Black Lick Creek section of country, back of Ninevah. The town of Armagh is two miles from this station.

Florence, Philadelphia, 291 miles; Pittsburgh, 65 miles.
Express, on time, going West, stops; East stops.
Mail, on time, going West, stops; East stops.

An outlet for Centreville, a small town located a short distance on the river. From Florence roads diverge to Ligonier, and other towns on the South, and to Indiana on the North.

Lockport, Philadelphia, 296 miles; Pittsburgh, 60 miles.
Mail, on time, going West, stops
The road from this point is double track.

Bolivar, Philadelphia, 297 miles; Pittsburgh, 59 miles.
This station is located near a defile in Chestnut Ridge, through which the road passes. The scenery in this gorge is characterized by a bold beauty that rarely fails to delight.

Blairsville Branch Intersection, Philadelphia, 302 miles;
Pittsburgh, 54 miles.
Express, on time, going West, stops. East, stops.
Mail, on time, going West, stops. East, stops.

Blairsville and Indiana Branch.

Distance to Blairsville, 3 miles; Indiana, 19 miles. Trains leave Intersection for Blairsville 7.25 and 10.30, A M. and 6,05 P. M.
Returning, leaves for Intersection 6.55 and 9:30 A. M., and 5.25, P. M.
Trains leave Intersection for Indiana, 10.30, A. M. and 6.05 P. M.
Returning, leave Indiana for Intersection, 5.35, A. M. and 3,50, P M.

Blairsville is situated in Indiana County, three miles from the Intersection on the Conemaugh, immediately above Black Lick Creek. It is 40 miles by the Northern Turnpike, on which it lies, from Pittsburgh. . It was laid out about 1812, and has now a population of about 2000

INDIANA, is the capital of Indiana County ; it is 19 miles from the intersection, and is the terminus of the branch road. Its population is about 1,500. It was laid out in 1805. There are said to be traces of one of those ancient fortifications, which are scattered throughout the west, to be seen about three miles south-west of the town.

Hillside, Philadelphia, 306 miles; Pittsburgh, 50 miles.
Mail, going West, stops 4 m.
A Wood and Water Station on the western slope of Chestnut Ridge.

Millwood, Philadelphia, 308 miles; Pittsburgh, 48 miles.
Flag Station.   Trains stop when signaled, or when passengers desire to get off.

Derry, Philadelphia, 310 miles; Pittsburgh, 46 miles.
Mail, going West, stops.
This station is about one mile south of the village of that name.

Saint Clair, Philadelphia, 312 miles; Pittsburgh, 44 miles.
Mail, going West, stops.

Latrobe, Philadelphia, 315 miles; Pittsburgh, 41 miles.
All Trains stop.   Wood and water Station.
Stages from this point to Youngstown.

This town was laid out a few years since, by Oliver W. Barnes, Esq. It is located on a fork of the Loyalhanna river, which the road crosses at this point.   There are several manufacturing establishments here.   There is a fine depot hotel here. and good fishing and shooting in the vicinity.

Beatty's, Philadelphia, 317 miles; Pittsburgh, 39 miles.
Mail, going West, stops.
The Roman Catholic Abbey of St. Vincent, is in the vicinity of this station.   After leaving this station, the road passes through two tunnels, from the last of which, the road emerges in full view of Greensburgh, Westmoreland county.

Greensburg, Philadelphia, 225 miles; Pittsburgh, 31 miles
All trains stop.   Stages leave this point for Mt. Pleasant, Somerset, Uniontown, Pa. and Cumberland, Md.

This town was laid out soon after the Indians had burned Hanna's Town, in 1782 ; and was incorporated as a borough in 1799.   The population at the present time, is about 2500, and the railroad has, of late years, given a fresh impetus to the place. In the Presbyterian church yard, of this borough, repose the remains of Gen. Arthur St. Clair, of revolutionary fame. At Ludwick, in the environs of the town, is the station for receiving and forwarding the freight of the town, and the surrounding country.

Radebaugh, Philadelphia, 327 miles; Pittsburgh, 29 miles.
Mail going West, stops.

Grapeville, Philadelphia, 329 miles; Pittsburgh, 27 miles.
Flag Station.   Accommodation Trains stop.

This station is an outlet for a village of the same name one mile north.

Manor, Philadelphia, 330 miles; Pittsburgh, 26 miles.
Mail, on time, going West, stops.

Irwins, Philadelphia, 334 miles; Pittsburgh, 22 miles.

From 400 to 500 tons of coal are shipped daily, from this station, by the Westmoreland Coal Company, to Philadelphia and New York, for gas.

Larimer's, Philadelphia, 336 miles; Pittsburgh 20 miles.
Mail, on time, going West, stops.

This station is also the outlet of extensive coal operations.

Stewart's, Philadelphia, 339 miles; Pittsburgh, 17 miles
Mail, on time, going West, stops.

Wall's, Philadelphia, 342 miles; Pittsburgh, 14 miles.
Flag station.   Accommodation Trains only stop
An Accommodation Train. which leaves Pittsburgh at 6:40 and 11:40 A. M. and 4.20. and 6.20 P. M. returning, leaves Walls' at 5.40 and 7:40. A. M. and 12.50 and 5:15 P. M.

This station is on Turtle Creek, the first station of the road going West, in Allegheny county.

Turtle Creek, Philadelphia, 343 miles; Pittsburgh, 13 miles.
Mail, on time, going West, stops.

Station named after the creek, which at this point runs along the road.

Brinton's, Philadelphia, 344 miles; Pittsburgh, 12 miles.
Mail, on time, going West, stops.

Braddocks, Philadelphia, 346 miles; Pittsburgh, 10 m.
Only Accommodation Trains stop here.

This station is immediately at the scene of Braddock's defeat. The facts of that disaster to the British arms, are too well known through history, to need mention here. The locality of the battle is now laid out in a village, known by the same name as the station, and but few of the original features of the landscape remain. The battle took place between the railroad and the river.

Swissvale, Philadelphia, 348 miles; Pittsburgh, 8 miles.
Only Accommodation Trains stop here.

In the neighborhood of this station are located the residences of many of the business men of Pittsburgh. The station is named for Jane G. Swisshelm, celebrated from her woman's rights teachings, who resided in this vicinity many years.

Wilkinsburg, Philadelphia, 349 miles; Pittsburgh, 7 miles.
Only Accommodation Trains stop here.

The vicinity of this station is also thickly dotted with the suburban houses of the merchants and manufacturers of Pittsburgh. The town derives its name from Hon. William Wilkins, a venerable statesman, and a distinguished son of Allegheny county, whose beautiful country seat is in the vicinity.

Homewood, Philadelphia, 350 miles; Pittsburgh, 6 miles.
Flag station. Accommodation Trains only stop when signaled, or when passengers desire to get off.

The station receives its name from the country seat of Hon. Wm. Wilkins.

East Liberty, Philadelphia, 351 miles; Pittsburgh, 5 miles.
Mail and Accommodation Trains only stop here.

This thriving village was laid out about forty years ago, by Jacob Negley, Esq. Of late years, the village has largely increased, in consequence of numbers of Pittsburgh business men making it their place of residence.

Millvale, Philadelphia, 354 miles; Pittsburgh, 2 miles.
Flag Station. Trains stop when signaled.

Outer Depot, (Pittsburgh,) of the Pennsylvania Railroad.

Just before reaching this, the beautifully located grounds and buildings o the Western Pennsylvania Hospital, may be seen on the left, going west. The grounds of the Outer Depot consist of about twenty acres, upon which is located a great variety of buildings, necessary to the transaction of the business of the Company. Among these buildings, is a local freight house, 300 feet long, and a circular engine-house, 900 feet in circumference, one of the largest buildings of its kind in the United States.

Pittsburgh, Philadelphia, 356 miles.

Trains running out of Pittsburgh leave as follows:—

Pennsylvania Central Road.

Express, 4:00, P. M., arriving at Philadelphia 6:35, A. M
Fast, 8:45, P. M.   "   "   "   10:20, A. M
Mail, 3:00, A. M.   "   "   "   5:25, P. M.
Johnstown Accommodation, leaves at 2:55 P. M., arriving at Johnstown, 7:18, P. M.
Local Accommodation, running to Wall's Station, leaves at 6:40, and 11:40, A. M. and 4:20 and 6:20, P. M.

Pittsburgh Ft. Wayne and Chicago Road.

Mail leaves at 7:00, A. M., arriving at Crestline 6:00, P. M.
Express " 12:40, P. M.,   " " Chicago 8:00, P. M.
Fast Line " 1:00, A. M.,   " " " 8:50, P. M.
Brighton Accommodation, leaves at 9:30, A. M., 4:20, P. M.
Economy   "   10:50, A. M., 5:40, P. M.

Cleveland, and Pittsburgh Road.

Mail Trains leaves at 1:00 A. M and 12:40, P. M.

Pittsburgh and Connelsville Road.

	Leave Pitts.	Ar. at Pitts.
Mail to and from Uniontown,	7:55 A. M.	6:00 P. M.
Express do do	3:40 P. M.	9:20 A. M.
1st M'Keesport Accommodation,	11:00 A. M.	6:50 A. M.
2d do do	6:15 P. M.	2:05 P. M.
Port Perry, do	7:00 P. M.	8:30 P. M.
2d do do	4:25 P. M.	6:05 P. M.
Sunday Church train to and from M'Keesport,	1:00 P. M.	10:00 A. M.

Allegheny Valley Road.

Mail Train leaves Pitts 7:00 A. M., arrives at Kittaning 10:00, A. M., returning leaves Kittaning 4:00, P. M. arrives at Pittsburgh 7:00, P. M.

Express Train leaves Kittanning at 6:50, A. M., arrives at Pitts at 9:35 A. M. Leaves Pitts. 3:40, P. M., arrives at Kittanning 6:50 P. M.

Accommodation Train leaves Soda Works at 5:00, A. M., arrives at Pitts. 8:00 A. M. Leaves Pitts. at 4:45, P. M., arrives at Soda Works at 7:05 P. M:

The City of Pittsburgh whose name has become synonymous with manu-turing industry and enterprise, may be said to have been originally a French ttlement, Monsieur Contrecour erecting Fort Duquesne in 1754, at the junc-n of the two rivers. The French regime was brief. In 1758 the French fire to and abandoned the Fort, upon the approach of Gen. Forbes, who mediately repaired the works and called them Fort Pitt; from whence ori-iated the name of Pittsburgh.

The community generally known as Pittsburgh, consists of twelve distinct inicipalities, and six villages or settlements, in addition, so immediately ning these, as to render it impossible for any but surveyo s to say where corporate municipalities end, and the minor villages commence. To angers they but appear the further extension of one or more streets. The tinct corporations consist of the cities of Pittsburgh and Allegheny; the roughs of Birmingham, East Birmingham, South Pittsburgh, Monongahe-Sligo, West Pittsburgh, Temperanceville, Manchester, Duquesne and Law-iceville—and the villages are Minersville, Oakland, Brownstown, Mount ishsngton, Hatfield and Woodland. The population of this thickly settled a of dwellings cannot be accurately given from any of the Census returns each of the cities and boroughs named, are separately counted in the umerations; and the difficulty is still further increased that a large mass the population is given in the enumerations of some of the surrounding wnships, into which the city's paved and closely built streets extend. From few census returns of this vicinity which have been made public, we be-ve the population of the community known as Pittsburgh, consisting of 12 corporations named, and their immediately adjoining villages, will not l short of 120,000, being an increase of 40,000 in ten years, or full 50 per it. To this increase of population, one inciting cause has been the geographi- advantages of the position. Located at the head waters of the Ohio, tsburgh commands an inland navigation of eleven thousand miles, through territory of fifteen States. But a few hours railroad ride from the Lakes, e partakes of their advantages for intercourse with the Canadas, or for an tlet by that route to the Ocean, distant but a summer day's journey, from ree important seaboard cities, she enjoys many of the business advantages cities lying immediately upon the sea coast. Another cause is her great vantages as a manufacturing city. Located in the heart of the bituminous al fields, she possesses immense supplies of cheap fuel; the coal used by r manufacturers costing only 80 cents per ton. Surrounded by the iron deposits of four states, she has copious and cheap supplies of that mineral, while the lead of the upper Mississippi, and the copper of Lake Superior, from her great transportation facilities, are easily and cheaply laid down at her work shops. Woods of all descriptions, indigenous to the country, are copiously, easily, and cheaply available from various sources.

To the enumeration of the leading manufactories, resulting from the great advantages so briefly sketched, we devote a paragraph. There are daily working in Pittsburgh, twenty-three rolling mills for iron, and three making and rolling steel exclusively. Forty-three founderies for casting iron, and five for brass. Seventeen steam engine and machine shops, and eight boiler yards. Three large manufactories of axes, vices, shovels, &c., and one of saws. Two heavy forges. One railroad spike factory, and two of hot pressed nuts. Three iron railing factories, three file factories, two of saddlery hard ware, one of boiler and other rivets, and one of wire. Two large manufactories of gun barrels, one of rifles, and one of repeating pistols. Two very heavy establishments devoted to the manufacture of domestic hardware, two iron safe factories, three of plows, and three of cutlery and surgical instruments. Two extensive rolling mills for copper. Five cotton, three red and white lead, and thirty-four glass factories. Four of looking glasses, two of railroad cars, two of Japan ware and pressed tin goods. Six of coaches, nine extensive ones, besides many small ones, of wagons. Thirty tanneries, thirty breweries of ale and of lager bier. Two steam cracker bakeries, six factories of lard and linseed oils, six potteries, three woollen factories, one of oil cloths, one of surveying and engineering instruments. Seventeen large tobacco factories, besides a number of small ones. Two patent leather manufactories, five flouring mills, and two spice mills. Sixteen extensive cabinet manufactories, besides quite a number on a limited scale. Two of varnish, two of paper, one of alchohol, one of kid gloves, three af brushes, four of trunks. Six large factories of saddlery and harness, besides many on a smaller scale; two of saddle-trees, two of whips and umbrellas, three of glue, eight very heavy of soap and candles, six of cut marble, two of buckets and tubs, three of kegs, one of Brittania ware, one of wire cloth, one of bells, one of procelain teeth, one of children's carriages, one of gold leaf, one of bobbins, one of corks, beside a great variety in all branches of industry usually prosecuted in a great city.

The number of houses in the two cities and boroughs, we have no estimate of, but in the city Directory we find the names of over three hundred and fifty streets. and one hundred and fifty alleys and courts recorded. Several of these streets are from three to four miles in length, and many from one to two miles long, closely built upon both sides. A number of the alleys are from a half to a mile in length, thickly lined with tenant houses. There are also mentioned in the Directory the names of over two thousand business firms, in the various branches of commerce, and the addresses of between three and four hundred professionals are given. There are eighteen chartered banks, and twelve private banking houses, twenty-nine public schools and three colleges twenty-five daily and weekly publications; thirty-four hotels, one theatre; twenty-five Odd Fellow's Lodges and ten of Ancient York Masons; eight public halls, seating from a thousand to twenty-five hundred persons each. Six railroads run daily to various parts of the Union.

There are three incorporated city passenger railway companies, whose roads starting from the heart of the city, pass up widely different routes to the four quarters of the city and suburbs. These roads vary in length from 3 to 5½ miles each, and running North, East, South and West in their course, afford great facilities to strangers to inspect the city and its suburbs at a trifling expense, besides furnishing nearly 40 miles of pleasant excursion. We subjoin the titles and course of the roads, with a brief mention of the leading objects of interest located along the route of each, as of assistance to the stranger who, while desirous of seeing something of the manufactures of Pittsburg brand its public places, may be equally anxious to economise his time.

CITIZEN'S PASSENGER RAILWAY.

Runs from the corner of St. Clair and Penn street, Pittsburgh to Sharps-burg, 5½ miles. Cars leave Penn street Station every 7¼ minutes, from 6.30 A. M., until 11.00 P. M.

Strangers desiring to inspect the City of Pittsburgh, will find this line affords fine facilities for visiting manufacturies, public works and institutions, as many of the most attractive are located along the line of this road. Among the attractive manufacturies and public places lying on either side of this Passenger Railway, are

THE ALLEGHENY CEMETRY, ALLEGHENY ARSENAL, CITY WATER WORKS, FAIR GROUNDS, IRON CITY PARK, WESTERN PENNSYLVANIA HOSPITAL, RAILROAD DE-POTS, LAKE SUPERIOR SMELTING WORKS & COPPER MILL, HUSSEY WELLS & CO.'S STEEL WORKS, FORT PITT CANNON FOUNDRY, FULTON IRON FOUNDRY, JUNIATA ROLLING MILL, PITTSBURGH ROLLING MILL, ÆTNA STOVE WORKS, DUQUESNE STEEL WORKS, O'HARA GLASS WORKS.

PITTSBURGH AND EAST LIBERTY PASSENGER RAILWAY.

Runs from corner of Market and Fourth street, to East Liberty, and, also, by a seperate route to Minersville. Cars leave the Fourth street Station every 15 minutes, from 6.55 A. M., until 10.30 P. M., to Oakland and Min-ersville, each alternate car runs through to East Liberty, being one every 30 minutes.

Strangers stopping at Pittsburgh for a season, will find the route of this road a charming one, passing as it does through a section of the suburbs, in which are situated many of the dwellings of the wealthier business men of the city, whose finely improved grounds and elegant residences enliven the beautiful natural valley through which the road runs. The visitor at Pittsburgh, who fails to visit this section of the suburbs and the adjacent village of East Liberty, neglects to see the fair, smiling side of the Smoky City, and does the city injustice, however much he may wonder at our immense manufacturies, in not also receiving impressions of taste and elegance from as fair a garden spot as any city can boast of

BIRMINGHAM AND PITTSBURGH PASSENGER RAILWAY.

Runs from Fifth to Smithfield street, Pittsburgh, to Brownstown, passing through South Pittsburgh, Birmingham and East Birmingham. Cars leave Smithfield street every 10 minutes, from 6.30 A. M., until 11 P. M.

This road, between 3 and 4 miles in length, affords to the stranger an agreeable ride, passing over the fine Wire Suspension Bridge across the Monongahela, a desirable view is obtained down the Ohio and up the Monongahela rivers. The road passes through a large manufacturing district, in which are located, among others, the following manufacturies :

WILLINGER'S PLANING MILLS, HIAWATHA NUT FACTORY, ROBINSON, MINNIS & MIL-LER'S FOUNDRY, DILWORTH'S RAILROAD SPIKE FACTORY, CHAMBER'S WINDOW GLASS WORKS, M'KEES' GLASS WORKS. RRYCE. RICHARDS & CO.'S FLINT GLASS WORKS, WOLFF, PLUNKET & CO.'S WINDOW GLASS WORKS, CUNNINGHAM'S WIN-DOW GLASS WORKS, HOLLMAN & GARRISON'S CHILLED ROLL FOUNDRY. M'KNIGHT'S ROLLING MILL. CHESS. SMITH & CO 'S TACK FACTORY, ORMSBY S COAL WORKS, AMERICAN IRON WORKS.

In concluding this enumeration of the leading pursuits of Pittsburgh, we subjoin the names of a few firms in a variety of the mercantile and manufacturing pursuits of the city, such information being at all times acceptable—and very often extremely desirable to the traveller, whether a dealer or consumer.

AXES, SHOVELS & SAWS.
Lippincott & Co., 118 Water

ALE.
Edmunds & Co., agents for Smith's Wheeling Ale, 21 Smithfield

AUCTIONEERS.
T. A. McClelland & Co., 55 Fifth

AXES, SHOVELS & HOES.
Newmyer, Graff & Co., 108 Water

ALDERMAN.
Alex. S. Nicholson, 69 Grant st., near Court House.

BANKERS.
Hill & Co., cor. 5th and Wood
N. Holmes & Sons, 57 Market
Kountz & Mertz, 118 Wood

BOOKSELLERS, STATIONERS & BLANK BOOK MANUFACTURERS.
Kay & Co., 55 Wood

BOOKS, STATIONERY AND NEWS DEALERS.
Charles C. Mellor, 81 Wood
Robt. S. Davis, 93 Wood

BOOTS AND SHOES, WHOLESALE.
H. Childs & Co., 133 Wood
W. E. Schmertz & Co., 31 Fifth

BRASS FOUNDRIES.
Maffet & Old, 127 First
Davis & Phillips, 110 Water

CARBON AND LUBRICATING OIL MANUFACTURERS.
Sellers, Canfield & Co., corner Wood and Second
Long, Miller & Co., 23 Market
W. P. Wooldridge, (Lucifer oil,) 39 Market
W. Mackeown, 167 Liberty
S. M. Kier & Co., Liberty oppo. Depot
Ardesco Oil Co., 27 Irwin
Geo. W. Holdship & Co., 35 Bank Block, Fifth
Kehew, McFadden & Co., 26 Market

Warden & Brooks, 14 Water
Brewer, Burke & Co., cor. Duquesne Way and Hancock, agent for Globe, Pacific and Liberty Oil Works
Richardson, Harley & Co., 19 Irwin
Clark & Sumner, 24 Wood
Wightman & Anderson, Eagle Works, 92 Third
W. A. McClurg, 61 Wood
J. F. Marshall, 139 Liberty
Reamer, Hays & Co., 281 Liberty
R. Ashworth, cor. St. Clair and Duquesne Way
Naylor & Smith, 41 Market, Wm. Logan, Agent

CARBON, CRUDE, LUBRICATING OILS AND BENZOLE DEALERS.
W. P. Logan, 41 Market
McClelland & Davis, 27 Wood
Childs & Carson, 38 Wood, under St. Charles Hotel
Robt. Wray, Jr., 4 Hand, at Hill's office
Wade Hampton, cor. Penn and Hand
J. F. Duncan & Co., 16 Hand

CARBON AND COAL OILS.
Lucesco Oil Co., 11 Wood
North American Oil Co., 80 Third

CARBON OIL LAMPS.
W. N. Ogden & Co., 64 Market
Wightman & Anderson, 92 Third

COOK, PARLOR AND HEATING STOVES
A. Bradley, cor. Wood and Second

CHILLED ROLL MANUFACTURERS.
Bollman & Garrison, 119 Smithfield

CARRIAGE MANUFACTURERS.
C. West & Co., 197 Penn

DRY GOODS, WHOLESALE.
Wilson, Carr & Co., 94 Wood
McCandless, Jamison & Co. 103 Wood
Arbuthnot, Shannon & Co., 115 Wood

DUFF'S COMMERCIAL COLLEGE,
Iron Buildings, 37 Fifth

FLINT GLASS WARE.
Jas. B. Lyon & Co., 116 Water
Bryce, Richards & Co., 41 Wood
Atterbury, Reddick & Co. cor. Carson
and McKee street, Birmingham

FOUNDERS AND MACHINISTS.
Bollman & Garrison, 119 Smithfield

FURNITURE MANUFACTURERS.
James W. Woodwell, 97 & 99 Third

GLUE CURLED HAIR AND BONE DUST.
A. Hoveller & Co., 15 Virgin alley

GROCERS.
Means & Coffin, cor. Wood and Water
J. S. Dilworth & Co. 130 & 132 Second
Little & Trimble, 112 and 114 Second

GAS AND WATER PIPE.
Spring, Chalfant & Co., (Wro't Iron)
91 and 92 Water

HATS, CAPS AND LADIES' FURS.
Wm. Fleming, 139 Wood

HIDE AND LEATHERS.
J. R. McCune, 181 Liberty

HARDWARE.
Wm. S. Lavely, 58 Wood
B. Wolff, Jr., cor. Liberty & St. Clair

HOT PRESSED NUTS, BOLTS AND WASHERS.
Knap, Wood & Co., 114 Water

IRON AND NAIL MANUFACTURERS.
Zug & Painter, 96 Water
Jones & Laughlin, 120 Water
Lyon, Shorb & Co., 121 Water
Lloyd & Black, 88 Water

IRON—GALVANIZED SHEET.
Moorhead & Co., 99 Water

IRON CITY COMMERCIAL COLLEGE.
Cor. Penn and St. Clair, opposite St. Clair Hotel

JEWELRY AND MILITARY GOODS.
H. Richardson & Co., cor. Fifth and Market

LOOKING GLASSES,
J. J. Gillespie, 88 Wood

MINERAL WATER MANUFACTURER.
J. C. Buffum, 26 Market

NAILS, TACKS AND BRADS.
Chess, Smith & Co., 112 Water

OIL BARRELS, MANUFACTURER.
Guthrie & Sill, 61 Water, & 64 Front

OIL CLOTH MANUFACTURERS.
J. & H. Phillips, 26 and 28 St. Clair

PIANOS AND MUSICAL GOODS.
C. C. Mellor, (Chickering & Sons and Hazleton & Bros. Pianos, and Mason & Hamlin's Melodeons,) 81 Wood
Kleber & Bro., (Steinway's Pianos and Carhart & Needham's N. Y. Melodeons,) 53 Fifth

PLOWS AND PLOW CASTINGS.
Hall & Speer, 166 Penn
J. C. Bidwell, cor. Duquesne Way, Fayette and Garrison alley
John Hall & Co., 139 Liberty

PAPER HANGINGS.
W. P. Marshall, 87 Wood

PLUMBERS, GAS & STEAM FITTERS.
Tate & Seville, 227 Liberty

PITTS. AGRICULTURAL WORKS.
Robt. S. Williams, (Manager,) 48 and 51 Ferry

PLANING MILLS, SASH AND DOORS.
John Heath, cor. Marbury and Duquesne Way

STEEL AXES & SPRINGS.
Hailman, Rahm & Co., 77 Water

SEWING MACHINES.
R. Straw, (Agent Singer's Machines,) 32 and 34 Market
A. McGregor, (Ag't Howe's Machines) cor. Penn and St. Clair
Wm. Sumner & Co., (Agent Wheeler & Wilson's,) 27 Fifth

TRIMMINGS AND STRAW GOODS.
Jos. Horne & Co., 77 and 79 Market.

WAGON MANUFACTURERS.
Phelps, Park & Co., 6 St. Clair

WOOL DEALERS.
J. W. Marshall, 139 Liberty.

WINDOW GLASS AND GLASS WARE.

A. & D. H. Chambers, 117 Water and 154 First

Cunningham & Co., 109 Water and 140 First

Geo. A. Berry & Co., 97 First

W. M'Cully & Co., 14 and 16 Wood

ALLEGHENY.

FLOUR MILLS.

J. L. Noble & Co., Pitt alley, near Diamond

MACHINISTS.

R. W. White & Bro., (wood-working machines,) West Common

OIL BARREL MANUFACTURERS.

Gregg, Alexander & Co., (J. Logan, manager,) river bank below Wire Bridge

PLUMBERS, GAS AND STEAM FITTERS,

Bailiff & Brown, 55 Federal

PLANING MILLS, SASH AND DOORS,

Gregg & Dalzell, cor. Main and Cherry

Leaving Pittsburgh the traveler pursues his way, after changing cars at the Union Depot of the two roads, by the Pittsburgh, Fort Wayne & Chicago Railway, the time table of which road and descriptions of its stations immediately follow, on page 46.

---

(44)

Pittsburgh, Fort Wayne & Chicago

RAILWAY.

G. W. CASS, President, Pittsburgh.

HON. SAM'L HANNA, Vice President, Fort Wayne.

JNO. B. JERVIS, General Superintendent, Pittsburgh.

T. D. MESSLER, Comptroller, Pittsburgh.

JNO. P. HENDERSON, Treasurer.

W. H. BARNES, Secretary, Pittsburgh.

JNO. J. HOUSTON, General Freight Agent, Pittsburgh.

WM. P. SHINN, General Passenger Agent, Pittsburgh

AUG'S BRADLEY, Superintendent Eastern Division,
Pittsburgh.

H. A. GARDNER, Supt., W. D., Ft. Wayne.

JOS. H. MOORE, Commercial and General Agent, Chicago.

TIME TABLE PITTSBURGH, FT. WAYNE & CHICAGO RAILWAY.

By Columbus Time, 13 minutes slower than Pittsburgh, and 20 minutes
faster than Chicago time.

TRAINS GOING WEST LEAVE STATIONS AS FOLLOWS:

LEAVES	CHI. EXP. P. M.	U. S. MAIL. A. M.	CHI. EXP. A. M.	CRES. ACCO. P. M.	LEAVE	NIG'T EXP. P. M.	MAIL ACCO. A. M.	DAY EXP. A. M.	CIN. EXP.
PITTSBURG	12 40	7 00	1 00	2 30	Crestline.....	8 30	5 00	8 30	
Allegheny....	12 50	7 10	1 10	2 40	Bucyrus......	9 00	5 33	8 58	
Haysville.....	......	7 39	......	3 36	Nevada.......	......	......	......	
Sewickley....	......	7 43	......	3 44	U. Sandusky	9 44	6 24	9 38	
Economy.....	......	7 57	......	4 10	Forest..	10 13	7 00	10 07	
Remington...	......	......	......	4 30	Dunkirk.......	......	......	......	
Rochester....	1 55	8 25	2 15	4 50	Washington.	......	......	......	
N. Brighton..	2 02	8 36	......	5 10	Johnstown...11 02		7 50	......	
New Gallilee		9 10	......	5.45	Lima..........11 39		8 39	11 33	
Enon..........	2 40	9 25	2 56	6 04	Delphos 12 15		9 22	12 06	
Palestine....:	......	9 40	......	6 20		A. M.		P. M.	
N. Waterford		9 53	......	6 35	Van Wert....12 49		10 04	12 38	
Columbiana..	3 15	10 09	......	6 55	Convoy.......	......	......	......	
Franklin.....	......	10 28	......	7 15	Monroeville..	......	......	......	
Salem	3 39	10 38	3 43	7 30	F.Wayne,Ar.	2 10	12 00	1 50	
Damascus....	......	10 56	......	7 48			P. M.		
Smithfield....	......	11 02	......	7 55	" Le.	2 15	12 15	2 10	
Alliance, Ar.	4 10	11 20	4 10	8 10	Coesse.........	......	......	......	
					A. M.	Columbia ...	3 02	1 22	2 53	
" Le.	4 30	11 40	4 15	6 40	Huntsville ...	......	......	......	
		P. M.			Pierceton....	3 28	1 58	......	
Strasburg....	......	12 05	......	7 02	Warsaw..:....	3 50	2 26	3 41	
Louisville....	......	12 25	......	7 28	Bourbon......	4 22	3 10	......	
Canton........	5 09	12 50	5 00	8 00	Inwood.......	......	......	......	
Massillon.....	5 25	1 17	5 17	8 34	Plymouth....	4 50	3 48	4 39	
Lawrence....		1 43	......	9 06	Hamlet.......	......	......	......	
Fairview... ..	......	1 57	......	9 24	Hanna.........	5 42	5 02	......	
Orrville.......	5 55	2 12	5 46	9 40	Wanatah......	......	......	......	A. M.
Wooster Su't		......	......	9 55	Valparaiso...	6 18	7 10	5 56	5 45
Wooster......	6 20	2 52	6 10	10 12	Wheeler......	......	......	......	
Shreve........	......	3.32	......	10 34	Hobart.........	6 41	7 39	......	6 11
Lakeville.....		3 56	......	10 50	Liverpool..:...	......	......	......	
Loudonville..	7 04	4 18	6 52	11 10	Tollestone ...	......	......	......	
Perrysville...		4 33	......	11 25	Clarke.........	......	......	......	
Lucas.........		4 56	......	11 48	Robertsdale .	......	......	......	
				P. M.	Ainsworth...	......	......	......	
Mansfield.....	7 45	5 19	7 33	12 10	R. I. Junct'n,	7 35	8 43	......	7 15
Spring Mills.	......	......	......	12 25	Burlingt'n J.	7 50	9 00	7 25	7 30
Crestline......	8 15	6 00	8 00	12 50	Chicago...:...	8 00	9 10	7 35	7 40

TIME TABLE PITTSBURGH Ft. WAYNE & CHICAGO RAILWAY.

By Columbus time, 13 minutes slower than Pittsburgh and 20 minutes faster than Chicago time.

TRAINS GOING EAST LEAVE STATIONS AS FOLLOWS:

LEAVES	NIG'T EXP. P. M.	DAY EXP. A. M.	MAIL ACCO. A. M.	CIN EXP. P. M.
CHICAGO ...	7 35	7 40	4 20	8 50
Burlingt'n J.	7 45	7 5s	4 30	9 00
R. I. Junct'n	7 59	......	4 50	9 15
Robertsdale..	......	......	......	......
Clarke	......	......	......	......
Tollestone ...	......	......	......	......
Hobart	8 59	......	6 11	10 20
Valparaiso...	9 25	9 20	7 00	10 45
Wanatah	......	......	......	
Hanna	9 57	......	7 45	
Hamlet	......	......	......	
Plymouth ...	10 55	10 46	8 58	
Bourbon	11 19	......	9 31	
Etna Green..	......	......	......	
Warsaw	11 49	11 37	10 14	
	A. M.	P. M.		
Pierceton	12 09	......	10 41	
Columbia ...	12 38	12 24	11 18	
Coesse	......	......	......	
			P. M.	
F. Wayne, Ar.	1 20	1 05	12 15	
" Le.	1 25	1 25	12 30	
Monroeville..	......	......	......	
Dixon	......	......	......	
Van Wert....	2 43	2 42	2 02	
Middle Point	......	......	......	
Delphos	3 14	3 13	2 41	
Elida	......	......	......	
Lima	3 49	3 50	3 27	
Lafayette	......	......	......	
Johnstown...	4 27	......	4 13	
Washington,	......	......	......	
Dunkirk	......	......	......	
Forest	5 10	5 13	5 03	
U. Sandusky	5 42	5 45	5 50	
Nevada	......	......	......	
Bucyrus	6 19	6 22	6 37	
Crestline	6 45	6 50	7 10	

	CHI. EXP. A. M.	CHI. EXP. P. M.	CIN. EXP. P. M.	U. S. MAIL. A. M.
Crestline	7 05	7 10	1 12	7 15
Spring Mills.	......	......	......	7 42
Mansfield	7 33	7 45	1 38	8 00
Lucas	......	......	......	8 22
Perrysville	......	......	......	8 43
Loudonville..	8 15	8 24	2 15	9 00
Lakeville	......	......	......	9 18
Shreve	......	......	......	9 38
Wooster	9 10	9 10	2 52	10 12
Orrville	9 40	9 40	3 16	11 00
Fairview	......	......	......	11 10
Lawrence	......	......	......	11 21
Massillon	10 13	10 12	3 44	11 45
				P. M
Canton	10 33	10 30	3 59	12 10
Louisville	......	......	......	12 25
Strasburg	......	......	......	12 45
Alliance, Ar.	11 20	11 10	4 30	1 10
" Le.	11 40	11 15	4 45	1 25
Smithfield	......	......	......	1 50
Damascus	......	......	......	2 05
		P. M.		
Salem	12 15	11 44	5 14	2 30
Franklin	12 25	......	......	2 45
		A. M.		
Columbiana.	......	......	......	3 15
N. Waterford	......	......	......	3 34
Palestine	......	......	......	3 50
Enon	1 12	12 37	6 04	4 15
New Gallilee	......	......	......	4 35
N. Brighton..	1 45	......	6 36	5 10
Rochester	2 00	1 20	6 45	5 25
Remington	......	......	......	......
Economy	......	......	......	5 56
Sewickley	......	......	......	6 15
Haysville	......	......	......	6 21
Allegheny....	2 55	2 15	7 40	6 55
PITTSBURG	3 05	2 25	7 50	7 05

Accommodation Trains Pittsburgh, Ft. Wayne & Chicago Railway.

EASTERN DIVISION.

NEW BRIGHTON ACCOMMODATION

LEAVES ALLEGHENY

At 9:15 and 12:00 A. M. arriving at New Brighton, 11:15 A. M. and 1:45 P. M.
" 4:45 " 6:10 P. M. " " 6:30 " " 8:20 P. M.

LEAVES NEW BRIGHTON

At 5:00 and 6:30 A. M. arriving at Allegheny at 6:50 and 8:15 A. M.
" 12:20 " 2:50 P. M. " " 2:30 " 4:50 P. M.

WESTERN DIVISION.

CINCINNATI EXPRESS.

Leaves Valparaiso, 5:45 A. M., arrives at Chicago, 7:40 A. M.
Leaves Chicago, 8:50 P. M., " Valparaiso, 10:45 P. M.

CHICAGO & ROCK ISLAND JUNCTION ACCOMMODATION

Leaves Chicago, 8:15 A. M. arrives at R. I. Junction 8:45 A. M.
1:20 P. M. " " 1:50 P. M.
6:30 P. M. " " 7:00 P. M.

Leaves R. I. Junction at 6:55 A. M. arrives at Chicago 7:20 A. M.
12:00 M. " " 12:30 P. M.
5:50 P. M. " " 6:20 P. M.

The Pittsburgh, Ft. Wayne & Chicago Railway.

This is the most important trunk road in the West. Extending with great directness from Pittsburgh, through the states of Ohio and Indiana, to Chicago; the road acquires an importance not easily estimated from the number and extent.of the connections which it makes, with cross roads that concentrate upon it, from every section of Ohio, Indiana, and Illinois. This extent of connection, renders it not only the main channel down which pours in its course to the East, the flood of agricultural wealth of the Lake States and the Far West; but also a great distributor of the manufactured products and varied merchandise of the East; and likewise the best highway for the army of travel constantly traversing and re-traversing between the two sections of the country it connects. A direct and speedy route for those pushing through to extreme points, it is in the greatest degree convenient from the number of its cross connections before mentioned, for those dwelling at interior points, or whose business calls for frequent divergements, during their route, from the main line.

Running through a section of the Union remarkable for its fertility, and the enterprise and prosperity of its inhabitants, the frequency and variety of the towns and villages passed through, the bustle of life observable along the entire route, and the pleasant rural scenes presented to the eye, destroy the monotony of travel; while the speed of its trains, the comfortable appointment of its cars, and the certainty of its connections, greatly relieve its irksomeness.

The line of road which now forms the Pittsburgh, Fort Wayne and Chicago Railway, was originally three distinct roads, unfinished in their construction, and incomplete in the appointments of their working portions. Consolidated into the present trunk route, which has since been brought to its present usefulness and completion, draining in its direct route a total of 24 counties, producing 30,000,000 bushels of grain, with a population approaching 7,000,000, and by three of its principal connections between Pittsburgh and Chicago, 31 counties more, producing over 60,000,000 bushels of the several kinds of grain with a population of nearly 1,000,000; besides commanding its share of the immense business concentrated at Chicago by the system of railroads centering in that city. From the East by its direct connection with the magnificent road of the Pennsylvania Central Company, it presents to travel the shortest route to the North-West, and the most speedy, because direct in its connections, distributor of merchandise for western states. The first station on this road after leaving Pittsburgh, where its connection is made with the Pennsylvania Railroad..

Allegheny City: Chicago, 467 miles.

All the regular trains of the Pittsburgh Ft. Wayne & Chicago Railway stop at this Station, and leave viz: Mail West, 7:10, A. M., Express West, 1:10, A. M., Crestline Accommodation, 1:50 A. M , Cleveland and Pittsburgh Passenger, 6:10 A. M., New Brighton Accommodation, 9.15, 12.00, A. M., 4:45, 6:10, P. M., Cleveland and Pittsburgh Accommodation, 4:00, P. M.

The intimate relations which exist in the business of this city with Pittsburgh, naturally leads to much of its business being noticed in connection with that city. Of itself, it contains about 30,000 population, and is a rapidly growing city. A large number of manufactories are located within its jurisdiction, among which are five first class cotton factories, five heavy foundries, five machine shops, two first class merchant flouring mills, two oil mills, several agricultural implement manufactories, two woollen mills, a number of sash and door factories, and planing mills, besides a host of minor establishments. There are three banks in this city, and a large number of dry-goods and grocery houses, doing a heavy business, together with many others, in all the various branches of commerce. The city is well supplied with gas and water, from works erected on this side of the river for that purpose. Allegheny is finely situated, upon a succession of benches of level ground, and beautiful private residences abound throughout its limits.

Outer Station; Pittsburgh, 2 miles; Chicago, 466 miles.

The machine shops of the Pittsburgh, Fort Wayne & Chicago Railroad are located here. They are the largest on the whole line between Chicago and Pittsburgh. The first building was erected in 1850. The works give employment to two hundred men. At this point all the trains change engines.

Manchester. Pittsburgh, 3 miles; Chicago, 464 miles.

Sation for Accommodation trains only.

This station is the switch station of the Cleveland and Pittsburgh Railroad where that road branches off to go to its machine shop. It is named for the borough of Manchester, which it adjoins. The large building on the left, one fourth of a mile east of this station, is the U. S. Marine Hospital; while that near the station enclosed by a stone wall is the House of Refuge.

Courtney's, Pittsburgh, 7 miles; Chicago 461 miles. Station

for Accommodation trains only.

Dixmont, Pittsburgh, 8 miles; Chicago 459 miles.
Station for Accommodation trains only.

The Penna. Insane Asylum, an institute established by the philanthropic Miss. Dix, (after whom the station is named,) and built in 1860, is located upon the hill to the right.

Killbuck, Pittsburgh, 9 miles; Chicago, 458 miles.
Station for Accommodation trains only.

Haysville, Pittsburgh, 11 miles; Chicago, 457 miles.

Sewickley, Pittsburgh 12 miles; Chicago, 455 miles.
Station for Mail and Accommodation Trains.

Mail going West passes at 7:43, A. M.; going East 6:15, P M.
Express do do 1:40, P. M.; do 2:29, A. M.
Cincinnati Express " " 2:38, P. M., do 7:13, P. M.
New Brighton Accommodation leaves going West, 10:03, 12:47,
A. M., and 5:28, 7:06, P. M. ; going East, 6:04, 7:27, A. M.
and 1:36, 4:00, P. M.

This pleasant little town is seen to but little advantage from the depot, as it lies t ack of the brow of the hill. A large number of beautiful country residences are erected here, by persons doing business in Pittsburgh.

Edgeworth, Pittsburgh 13 miles; Chicago, 454 miles.
Station for Mail and Accommodation trains only.
The site of a flourishing Female Seminary is ¼ mile to the right, surround ed by a large settlement of suburban residences, &c.

Leetsdale, Pittsburgh 14 miles; Chicago, 453 miles.
Station for Mail and accommodation Trains.

From this station a lane leads to the ferry across the Ohio, to Shoustown on the left bank of that river.

Economy, Pittsburgh, 17 miles; Chicago, 450 miles.
Station for Mail and Accommodation trains only
New Brighton Accommodation leaves for Pittsburgh, 6:10, 7.35,
A. M. and 1:43, 2:43 P. M. Arrives at Economy from Pitts-
burgh, at 1:04, 10:24, A. M. and 5:49, 7:28, P. M.

The station is so called, from the town of Economy, situated on the hill above the station. The town of Economy is inhabited by a peculiar people, who hold all property in common, and discourage the intercourse of the sexes; the married members living as brothers and sisters. The society was originally formed by Mr. George Rapp, who, with his followers, emigrated from

Wirtemberg, in the province of Swabia, Germany, and arrived in the United States in 1803. They first settled at Harmony, in Butler County, but afterwards removed to Indiana. The climate not agreeing with them, in 1825 they returned to Pennsylvania, and located on the tract of land they still occupy. The society has become very wealthy from the results of their labors, notwithstanding several secessions which have taken place from their body. The society still carries on its affairs, in the same manner as when first organized.

Baden, Pittsburgh, 20 miles; Chicago, 447 miles.
Station for Mail and Accommodation trains only.

Remington; Pittsburgh, 22 miles; Chicago, 446 miles.
Station for Accommodation trains only.

Freedom. Pittsburgh, 24 miles; Chicago 444, miles.
Station for Mail and Accommodation trains only.

Rochester. Pittsburgh, 25 miles; Chicago, 442 miles.
All Trains stop.
Mail leaves going West 8:25 A. M.; East, 5:20 P. M.
Express leaves going West, 2:15 A. M.; East, 1:55 P.M.
Cin. Express leaves going West, 3:39 A. M.; East, 6:42 P. M.
Accommodation leaves for Pittsburgh, 5:10 and 6:42 A. M.; and 12:30 and 3:00, P. M.

Packets by Beaver and Erie Canal, for New Castle, and other points. Cleveland & Pittsburgh road branches off here to Bellaire.

At this point commences a series of small towns, clustered around the mouth of the Beaver river. They are Rochester, Bridgewater, Beaver, Sharon, New Brighton, and Brighton. The first settlement which was made in the neighborhood, was by the erection of Fort McIntosh, in 1778, near the site of Beaver. It was a strong stockade, with bastions mounting one six-pounder. In 1796, a tavern was opened near the fort, by Samuel Johnson. In 1803, a furnace was erected at the Falls, near Brighton, by Hoopes, Townsend & Co. In 1806, the second paper mill west of the mountains, was erected on Little Beaver Creek. About 1830 the vast natural advantages of the Falls of the Beaver, began to attract attention. A number of speculators laid hold of the sites, and under the impulse of speculative fever, lots were sold at enormous prices, manufactories were erected, hotels and beautiful dwellings were built, a branch of the United States' Bank established, and all went on merrily until the bubble burst. Much good, however, was done, and a large population of six or seven thousand persons was drawn around the Falls of the Beaver.

Beaver, Pittsburgh, 26 miles; Chicago, 441 miles.
Station for Accommodation trains only.

The bridge crosses the Beaver river from this station to Bridgewater and the Borough of Beaver, the county seat of Beaver Co., and the location of two female and one male seminary.

New Brighton. Pittsburgh, 29 miles; Chicago, 439 miles.

All trains, except night express, stop.
Mail going West leaves at 8:36, A. M.   Going East, 5:10, A. M.
Express, going West, leaves 2:02, P. M.   Going East, 1:45, P. M.
Cin. Express going West, leaves 3:51 A. M. going East 6:36 P. M.
Accom'd'n leaves for Pittsb'gh, 5:00, 6:30 A. M., 2:50, 12:20, P. M.
Leaves Pitts. for N. Brighton, 9:05,11:50 A. M., 3:50, 4:35 P. M.

There are a number of manufactories carried on at this point. A fine female university is located here, and a most excellent public school. The place is quite a popular resort for summer visiters. The society of the town is good. Passengers desiring to go up the Pittsburgh and Erie Canal, can take the packet boats at this point, as well as at Rochester. There was a military block-house established at this point in 1793. The water power at this place is unsurpassed.

Homewood, Pittsburgh, 37 miles; Chicago 430 miles.

Flag station for Mail and Accommodation trains.

New Gallilee. Pittsburgh, 40 miles; Chicago, 427 miles.

Mail and Accommodation only stop.

This place is sometimes called Darlington Station, being within two miles of old Darlington, and is the outlet for the business of that town. A railroad six miles in length, owned by the Economite society, proceeds from this point throughᵗ Darlington to the extensive cannel coal mines belonging to said society. The first establishment for the manufacture of coal oil, was erected here; and since its erection some ten or twelve others have been built in the immediate vicinity. This is also the junction of the New Castle and Nicholson's Run Railroad, about 14 miles long, yet unfinished. New Galilee owes its origin to the railroad, being built up since the road was corstructed. Population, about 200.

Enon. Pittsburgh, 45 miles; Chicago, 422 miles.

All Trains stop.

This station is 14 miles south of New Castle, the county seat of Lawrence County, for which place stages leave daily. Stages also leave daily for Poland and Youngstown. From Youngstown travelers take the cars on the Cleveland and Mahoning Valley Railroad to Warren, &c. on to Cleveland. Stages connect for New Castle, Mercer, Sharon and Youngstown with Mail and Express trains, going West, and arriving from these points, connect with Chicago Express and Cincinnati Express, East

Palestine. Pittsburgh, 50 miles; Chicago, 418 miles.

Station for Mail and Accommodation trains.

This town was laid out in 1832, and was originally called Mechanicstown.

New Waterford. Pittsburgh, 54 miles; Chicago, 413 miles.
Station for Mail and Accommodation trains.

Columbiana. Pittsburgh, 60 miles; Chicago, 407 miles.
Flag station for Express. Regular for Mail and Accommodotion trains.
This thriving town derives its name from Columbiana County, in which it is located. The county was settled just before the commencement of the present century, in 1797. The soil is excellent for agricultural purposes, and the tract abounds in coal, iron ore, and limestone. A large amount of business is transacted in the town, which contains machine shops, foundries and mills, three churches, two hotels, and about 2000 inhabitants.

Franklin. Pittsburgh, 66 miles; Chicago, 401 miles.
Station for Mail and Accommodation trains.

Salem. Pittsburgh, 70 miles; Chicago, 398 miles.
All Trains stop.
This flourishing town, which now contains about 4,000 population, was laid out in 1806, by members of the society of Friends, who came from Redstone, Pa., [now Brownsville.] The town is lighted with gas, and contains six churches. There are a number of machine shops and foundries carried on here, and a thriving business is done in most mercantile branches. Stages leave daily for Canfield, Warren, Mecca, and the Oil Regions.

Damascus. Pittsburgh, 76 miles; Chicago, 392 miles.
Station for Mail and Accommodation trains.
A growing town with 350 of a population. Coal and iron banks abound in this neighborhood.

Smithfield. Pittsburgh, 78 miles; Chicago, 390 miles.
Station for Mail and Accommodation trains.

Alliance, Pittsburgh, 83 miles; Chicago, 384 miles.
Night Express stops 5 m.
Mail, going West, stops 20 m; East, 20 m.
Day Expresses stop 20 min. for meals.
Trains for Cleveland leave Alliance, 6:35 A. M. and 4:45 P. M.
" " Wellsville " " 10:44 " " 3:55 "
This town is situated in Stark County, which was organized in 1809, and was named after General Starke, of revolutionary fame. At this station is a fine dining saloon, where passengers are allowed 20 minutes to dine. There is a large manufactory of agricultural implements carried on at this place. The track of the Cleveland and Pittsburgh Railroad crosses at this point, that of the Pitts. Ft. W. & Chicago road.

Strasburg. Pittsburgh, 89 miles; Chicago, 378 miles.
Mail and Accommodation stop.
This village is settled principally by French and Germans. It is in Stark Co.

Canton. Pittsburgh, 102 miles; Chicago, 366 miles.
All Trains stop.

This is the county seat of Stark County. The town was laid out in 1806. At the present time it has a population of about 7,000. There are a number of flouring mills in the vicinity, and two foundries in the town; also two extensive agricultural implement manufactories, giving employment to some 500 hands; seven churches, a magnificent graded public school, and a flourishing Female Institute. There is here located a branc'. of the State Bank of Ohio, a number of fine hotels, mercantile houses, &c Three newspapers are published, one German and two English, one of the latter being the oldest newspaper in the state of Ohio. Canton is growing rapidly and promises to eclipse all its immediate neighbors·in wealth, enterprise, numbers, &c.

Massillon. Pittsburgh, 109 miles; Chicago, 358 miles.
All Trains stop.

This bustling town is one of considerable note. There are in it three foundries, three machine shops, and one very extensive car manufactory, two blast furnaces, two very large agricultural implement manufactories, two large and fine hotels, besides a dozen smaller ones, a newspaper, a bank, seven churches, and many elegant und tasteful private residences. A large amount of wheat is annually shipped from this place. Extensive deposites of coal exist in the vicinity. The railroad crosses the Ohio Canal here. Massillon was laid out in 1828, and named for a celebrated French divine. The population is 4,000

Lawrence. Pittsburgh, 117 miles; Chicago, 351 miles.
Station for Mail and Accommodation trains.

Fairview. Pittsburgh, 121 miles; Chicago, 347 miles.
Station for Mail and Accommodation trains.

Orrville. Pittsburgh, 124 miles; Chicago, 344 miles.
All trains stop.

Orville is the junction of the Cleveland, Zanesville & Cin. R. R. Trains leave for Akron and Cleveland 6.07 A. M. and 2.43 P. M. For Millersburg 11.21 P. M. & 6.43 P. M.

At this point the Cleveland Zanesville and Cincinnati, Railroad crosses the Pittsburgh, Fort Wayne and Chicago road. The village contains about 500 inhabitants.

Wooster Summit. Pittsburgh, 129 miles; Chicago, 338 miles.
Station for Mail and Accommodation.

Wooster Pittsburgh, 135 miles; Chicago, 332 miles.
All trains stop.

The county seat of Wayne County, which was established in 1796, by proclamation of Governor St. Clair, and was the third county formed in the North West Territory. Its limits were originally very extensive, and embraced what is part of Ohio, Indiana, Illinois, Wisconsin and all of Michigan. Wooster was laid out in 1808, and named for Gen. David Wooster, an officer of the revolution. There were then no white inhabitants between it and the Lakes on the north ; on the west, none short of the Miami, Fort Wayne and Vincennes There is now a population of 4,000 in Wooster, and the town contains eleven churches, supported by as many different denominations· There are three foundries, two machine shops, one flouring mill, and several other manufacturing establishments carried on in the town, which is lighted with gas. Wooster is a heavy shipping point for grain, wool, and other produce.

Millbrook. Pittsburgh, 141 miles; Chicago, 326 miles.
> Station for Mail and Accommodation.

Shreve. Pittsburgh, 144 miles; Chicago, 323 miles.
> Station for Mail and Accommodation.

A thriving village of 250 inhabitants, located on Killbuck Creek.

Lakeville. Pittsburgh, 150 miles; Chicago, 317 miles.
> Station for Mail and Accommodation.

The place is named from a series of lakes, which are to be noticed on the left of the road, going west.

Loudonville. Pittsburgh, 156 miles; Chicago, 311 miles.
> All trains stop.

The town bearing this name contains four churches and 500 inhabitants.

Perrysville. Pittsburgh, 161 miles; Chicago, 307 miles.
> Station for Mail and Accommodation.

Lucas. Pittsburgh, 168 miles; Chicago, 299 miles.
> Station for Mail and Accommodation.

Mansfield, Pittsburgh, 175 miles; Chicago, 292 miles.
> All trains stop.

Mansfield is the Junction of the Sandusky, Mansfield & Newark R. R. Trains leave for Sandusky 7.35 A. M., 12.10 and 5.23 P. M. For Newark, 8.50 and 11.55 A. M.

This is the county seat of Richland County. The town was located in 1808. It is situated about 45 miles from Sandusky, and 25 miles from Mount Vernon. Mansfield is well laid out; is lighted with gas, and contains about 6,000 inhabitants. There are ten churches in the town, and three printing offices. Among other manufacturing establishments carried on here, there are three mills and two foundries.

Spring Mills. Pittsburgh, 180 miles; Chicago, 287 miles.
> Station for Mail and Accommodation.

Richland. Pittsburgh, 184 miles; Chicago, 284 miles.
Station for Mail and Accommodation.

Crestline. Pittsburgh, 188 miles; Chicago, 279 miles.
Express Trains all stop here 20 minutes.

Crestline is the Junction of the Cleveland Columbus and Cincinnati R. R. and the Bellefontaine R. R. Trains leave for Cleveland 6.35 A. M. and 1.05 and 6.35 P.M., for Cincinnati 8.30 A. M. and 8.40 P. M.

For Indianapolis and St. Louis 8.30 A. M. and 8.45 P. M. Passengers change cars for Columbus, Cincinnati, Indianapolis, Louisville and St. Louis.

This is one of the principal stations of the road. The company have extensive machine shops at this point, for repairing locomotives and cars. The town contains population of about 2,000.

Connections with Cincinnati, Indianapolis and St. Louis.

GOING WEST.			GOING EAST.		
Crestline..... 8:30 A. M.	8:40 P. M.		St. Louis....6.30 A.M.	455 P.M.	
Columbus...10:45 "	11:15 "		Louisville....245 P.M.	10:00 "	
Cincinnati....3.50 P. M.	5:55 A. M.		Indianapolis 8:15 "	5:00 A.M.	
Indianapolis..6:00 "	6:00 A. M.		Cincinnati..10:15 "	7:00 A.M.	10:15 A.M.
Louisville....12:50 A. M.	12:40 P. M.		Columbus...4:00 A.M.	11:10 "	3.45 P.M
St. Louis.... 8:10 A. M.	7:45 "		Crestline. ..6:35 "	1:05 "	6:35 P.M

Robinson. Pittsburgh, 195 miles; Chicago, 273 miles.
Flag Station for Mail Train.

Bucyrus. Pittsburgh, 201 miles; Chicago, 267 miles.
All trains stop.

This is the county seat of Crawford County. It is situated on the Sandusky river. The town was laid out in 1822, being first settled by a party of emigrants from Connecticut, on July 3d, 1821. It has now a population of some 1500. There are five churches in the town: also two foundries, one plough factory, one flour mill, and one steam saw-mill. In August, 1838, the skeleton of a mastodon was discovered near the site of the town. The head and skull-bones were perfect.

Nevada. Pittsburgh, 209 miles; Chicago, 258 miles.
Flag Station for Mail Train and Night Express.

This town is situated in a fertile, timbered county. A large quantity of fine lumber is shipped from this point. Population 150.

Upper Sandusky. Pittsburgh, 217 miles; Chicago, 250 miles.
All trains stop.

This flourishing town is the county seat of Wyandotte County, Indiana. Around its site cluster many interesting historical incidents. Three miles north of this town, on the road to Tiffin, is the locality of the battle between Col. Crawford and the Wyandotte Indians, at which he was captured, and afterwards burned, with terrible tortures, at the stake. The location where he suffered, is a few miles west of Upper Sandusky, on the old trace leading to the Big Spring, Wyandotte Town.

The present town was also the site of Fort Ferree, built by Gen. Harrison, during the war of 1812. One mile north was "The Grand Encampment" of Gov. Meigs, in August, 1813, with several thousand Ohio troops, on their way to the relief of Fort Meigs, then beseiged by the British forces.

The present town was laid out in 1843, and now contains a population of about 2000. There are several churches in the town, and the prosperity of the inhabitants is enhanced by the carrying on of several manufactories, in addition to the customary mercantile and mechanical pursuits of so large a country town. On the outskirts of the town is the Wyandotte Mission Church, erected in 1824, by government funds. In its burial grounds are entered the remains of John Stewart, first missionary to the Wyandottes; also the ashes of Sum-mun-de-wat, a noted chief and Methodist convert. Upper Sandusky is on the west branch of the Sandusky river, 63 milesfrom Columbus.

Kirby. Pittsburgh, 224 miles; Chicago, 243 miles.
Flag Station forMail Trains.

Forest. Pittsburgh, 229 miles; Chicago, 238 miles.
All trains stop.

Forest is the Junction of the Sandusky, Dayton and Cin. R. R. Trains leave for Sandusky 1.25, P. M.
For Dayton and Cincinnati, 10.45, A. M.

Passengers change cars far Bellfontaine, Springfield and Dayton; also Tiffin and Sandusky.

This station is in Hardin County. Population, about 100.

Dunkirk. Pittsburgh, 236 miles; Chicago, 231 miles.
Flag Station for Mail Trains.

Washington. Pittsburgh, 239 miles; Chicago, 229 miles.
Flag Station for Mail Trains.

Lafayette. Pittsburgh, 252 miles; Chicago, 215 miles.
Flag station for Mail Trains.

Johnstown. Pittsburgh, 246 miles ; Chicago, 222 miles.
Night Express and Mail stop.

Lima. Pittsburgh, 260 miles; Chicago, 207 miles.
All trains stop.
Passengers change cars at this station for Sidney, Piqua,
Troy, Dayton, Cincinnati, Toledo and Detroit.
Lima is the Junction of Dayton & Michigan R. R.   Trains
leave for Toledo 12.00 M. and 11.50 P. M.   For Dayton
and Cincinnati, 3.50 A. M., and 4.00 P. M.

Lima was laid out in 1831, and now contains about 3,000 inhabitants.   It
is the county-seat of Allen County.   The machine shops of the Dayton and
Michigan Railroad, are situated here.

Elida, Pittsburgh, 267 miles; Chicago, 201 miles.
· Flag Station for Mail Trains.

Delphos. Pittsburgh, 274 miles; Chicago, 193 miles.
All trains stop.

This town contains 1800 inhabitants.   The Miami Extension Canal passes
through it.   The town commands a wide extent of country which furnishes
a large amount of grain.

Middle Point. Pittsburgh, 280 miles; Chicago, 187 miles.
Flag Station for Mail Trains.

Van Wert. Pittsburgh, 287 miles; Chicago, 180 miles.
All trains stop.

This town was laid out in 1837, and now contains a population of about
2000.   The town derives its name from the county of which it is the county-
seat.   The site of the town was evidently, in former times, an Indian village.
The timber of the locality, when first settled by white men in 1825, was of
small growth, and there were a number of bark houses in a good state of pre-
servation.   The ridge upon which the town is built, is a subject of curiosity,
giving evidence, from its entire surface and general formation, that some vast
body of water had beat its waves upon its sandy beach, at this spot.

Convoy. Pittsburgh, 295 miles: Chicago, 173 miles.
Flag Station for Mail Trains.

Dixon. Pittsburgh, 300 miles; Chicago, 167 miles.
Flag Station for Mail Trains.

Monroeville, Pittsburgh, 304 miles; Chicago, 163 miles.
Flag Station for Mail Trains.

Maples, Pittsburgh, 310 miles; Chicago, 158 miles.
Flag Station for Mail Trains.

Fort Wayne, Pittsburgh, 320 miles; Chicago, 148 miles.
All trains stop. Day trains stop 20 m. for Dinner. Night trains
stop 5 m. to change engines.

Fort Wayne is the Junction of Toledo and Wabash Railway.
Trains for Lafayette and St. Louis 2.50 A. M. and 2.30 P. M. Passengers for Peoria via the Logansport Peoria and Burlington R. R.,
change cars here. Also for Logansport, Lafayette, Decatur, Springfield, and Quincy, Ill. Hannibal, and St. Joseph, Mo.

Fort Wayne, the capital of Allen County, is the largest town on the line of
road, between Pittsburgh and Chicago. It was once the principal seat of the
Miami Indians. The disastrous battle between Gen. Harmer and the Indians
in October, 1790, took place on the opposite side of the river, just below the
old Fort. The Fort, from which the town derives its name, was built by Gen.
Wayne, 1794. The city has now a population of about 12,000. Among its
evidences of prosperity, are four foundries and machine shops, one car factory, three flouring mills, three sash and door factories, and one plow factory.
It is surrounded by a fine agricultural district, and a heavy amount of grain is
shipped from this city to points south and east.

The P. F. W. & C. R. W. Co., have large shops located just east of the Depot, from which they have recently turned out a new freight car each day, in
addition to keeping up their current repairs.

The Toledo & Wabash R. R. Co., also, have their engine house and machine
shops a short distance west of the Depot. Both shops employ a large number of men, and add materially to the prosperity of the city.

The station house of the P. F. W. & C. R. W. Co., is a fine brick structure,
containing an eating house with lodging rooms attached. The office of the
Superintendent of the Western Division and his Assistant, is also in the east
end of the building.

Arcola, Pittsburgh, 328 miles; Chicago, 139 miles.
Flag Station for Mail Trains.

Coesse, Pittsburgh, 334 miles; Chicago 134 miles.
Flag Station for Mail Trains.

Columbia, Pittsburgh, 339 miles; Chicago, 129 miles.
All trains stop.

This place is known as Columbia City, and is the county-seat of Whitley County, Indiana. It is situated on Blue river, 20 miles west of Fort Wayne. It was laid out in 1840, and contains about 1200 inhabitants. Considerable grain and timber are shipped from this point. The principal part of the village lies about one-eighth of a mile north of the road.

Huntsville, Pittsburgh, 346 miles; Chicago, 121 miles.
Flag Station for Mail Trains.

This town is in Whitley County, Indiana. Population 150.

Pierceton, Pittsburgh, 351 miles; Chicago, 117 miles.
Station for Mail and Night Express only.

Near the head of Tippecanoe and Turkey Creeks in this county, after which the station is named, are a number of beautiful lakes, covering 2,500 acres of area.

Warsaw, Pittsburgh, 359 miles; Chicago, 108 miles.
All trains stop.

Stages leave daily for Goshen, Indiana, and intermediate points.

This town is the county-seat of Kosciusko County. It is finely situated on Tippecanoe river, near two of the beautiful lakes mentioned in connection with Kosciusko station. It has a population of 1600, and contains among other good edifices, two fine churches.

Etna Green. Pittsburgh, 369 miles; Chicago, 98 miles.
Flag Station for Mails.

Bourbon. Pittsburgh, 373 miles; Chicago, 94 miles.
Station for Mail and Night Express.

Lumber is abundant here, and extensive saw mills located here are constantly manufacturing it for market. The population of the town is about 500.

Inwood. Pittsburgh, 378 miles; Chicago, 90 miles.
Flag Station for Mail Trains.

Plymouth, Pittsburgh, 384 miles; Chicago, 84 miles.
All trains stop.
Stages leave for Logansport and South Bend, tri-weekly.
Plymouth is the Junction of the Cin. Peru & Chicago R. R.
Trains leave for La Porte at 5:20, P. M.

This is the county-seat of Marshall County. It is situated on Yellow river, twenty-five miles from its junction with the Kankakee. The town was first settled in 1834; and now contains about 2000 inhabitants. It is quite a large grain and lumber depot.

Donelson. Pittsburgh, 391 miles; Chicago, 77 miles.
Flag station for Mails.

Grovertown. Pittsburgh, 394 miles; Chicago, 73.
Flag Station for Mails.

Hamlet. Pittsburgh, 399 miles; Chicago, 69 miles.
Davis. Pittsburgh, 403; Chicago, 64 miles.
Flag Station for Mails.

Hanna. Pittsburgh, 408 miles; Chicago, 59 miles.
Station for Mail and Night Express.

Morgan. Pittsburgh, 412 miles; Chicago, 56 miles.
Flag Station for Mails.

Wanatah, Pittsburgh, 415 miles; Chicago, 53 miles.
Wanatah is the Junction of the Louisville, N. Albany and Chicago R. R.
Flag station for Mails.

Valparaiso. Pittsburgh, 424 miles; Chicago, 44 miles.
All trains stop.
Mails going West, stop 1 hour 24 minutes.

This town is the seat of justice of Porter County, Indiana. It was laid out in 1836. Its population is now about 2000. Two Collegiate Institutions are located here, one Methodist and one Presbyterian.

Wheeler. Pittsburgh, 431 miles; Chicago, 37 miles.
Flag Station for Mails.

Hobart. Pittsburgh, 434 miles; Chicago, 33 miles.
Day Express does not stop; all other trains stop.

This town is on Deep River, in Lake County, and has 250 inhabitants. A stage coach runs daily to Crown Point, 12 miles distant.

Liverpool, Pittsburgh, 437 miles; Chicago, 30 miles.
Flag Station for Mail and Cin. Express.

Tollestone. Pittsburgh, 441 miles; Chicago, 26 miles.
Flag Station for Mail and Cin. Express.

Clarke, Pittsburgh, 444 miles; Chicago 24 miles.
Flag Station for Mail and Cin. Express.

Game abounds in the vicinity of this station. A lake, one mile distant, is well stocked with pickerel and white fish.

Robertsdale. Pittsburgh, 452 miles; Chicago, 16 miles.
Flag Station for Mail and Cin. Express.

Ainsworth. Pittsburgh, 455 miles; Chicago, 12 miles.
Flag Station for Mail and Cin. Express.

Rock Island Junction Pittsburgh, 461 miles; Chicago, 7 m.
All trains stop except the Day Express.
Passengers change cars for Jolliet, Ottawa, Peoria, Rock Island, Davenport, Muscatine, Washington and Iowa City.
Junction with Chicago and Rock Island R. R.

Burlington Junction Pittsburgh, 466 miles; Chicago, 1 mile.
Express, on time, going West, stops; East, stops.
Mail, on time, going West, stops ; East, stops.
Crossing of Chicago, Burlington & Quincy Rail Road.

CHICAGO. Pittsburgh, 468 miles.

Connecting with the following Roads leaving Chicago for the South, West and North :

Illinois Central R. R., for Urbana, Mattoon, Centralia, Cairo, St. Louis and Memphis.

Trains leave at 8:30 A. M., and 10:00 P. M.
"   arrive at 8:15 "   "   8:45 "

Chicago & Rock Island R. R., for Peoria, Joliet, La Salle, Rock Island, Iowa City.

Trains leave at 9:00 A. M., and 8:30 P. M.
"   arrive at 6:30 "   " 6:15 "

Chicago, Burlington & Quincy R. R., for Galesburg, Burlington, Ottumwa, Council Bluffs, Quincy, St. Joseph and Kansas.

Trains leave at 8:30 A. M., and 8:15 P. M.
"   arrive at 6:30   "   "   6:15   "

Chicago & Alton R. R., for Joliet, Bloomington, Spring-field, Ill., Alton and St. Louis.

Trains leave Union Depot at 8:30 A. M., and 8:45 P. M.
"   arrive at   "   at 6:00   "   "   7:50   "

Galena & Chicago Union R. R., for Galena, Dunleith, Dubuque, Fulton, Cedar Rapids, Marshalltown, Cedar Falls, Free-port, Prairie du Chien, La Crosse and St. Paul.

Trains leave at 9:00 A. M., and 8:30 P. M.
"   arrive at 5:00   "   "   3:55   "

Chicago & North-Western R. R., for Madison, Fond du Lac, Janesville, Fort Howard, Prairie du Chien, La Crosse and St. Paul.

Trains leave at 8:45 A. M., and 8:30 P. M.
"   arrive at 5:50   "   "   5:50   "

Chicago & Milwaukie Rail Road, for Milwaukie, Ra-cine, Waukegan, Honcin, Fond du Lac, Fort Howard, La Crosse and St. Paul.

Trains leave at 8:45 A. M., and 8:30 P. M.
"   arrive at 8:30   "   "   5:50   "